D0899132

COLLEGE OF MARIN LIBRARY
COLLEGE AVENUE
KENTFIELD, CA 94904

Careers in Focus

METEOROLOGY

Ferguson's
An Infobase Learning Company

Careers in Focus: Meteorology

Copyright ©2011 by Infobase Learning

All rights reserved. No part of this book may be reproduced or utilized in any form or by any means, electronic or mechanical, including photocopying, recording, or by any information storage or retrieval systems, without permission in writing from the publisher. For information contact:

Ferguson's
An imprint of Infobase Learning
132 West 31st Street
New York NY 10001

Library of Congress Cataloging-in-Publication Data

Careers in focus. Meteorology.
    p. cm.
  Includes bibliographical references and index.
  ISBN-13: 978-0-8160-8033-5 (hardcover : alk. paper)
  ISBN-10: 0-8160-8033-X (hardcover : alk. paper)   1. Meteorologists—Vocational guidance—Juvenile literature.   I. Ferguson Publishing.   II. Title: Meteorology.
  QC869.5.C37 2010
  551.5023—dc22

                                                                    2010047930

Ferguson's books are available at special discounts when purchased in bulk quantities for businesses, associations, institutions, or sales promotions. Please call our Special Sales Department in New York at (212) 967-8800 or (800) 322-8755.

You can find Ferguson's on the World Wide Web at
http://www.infobaselearning.com

Text design by David Strelecky
Composition by Newgen
Cover printed by Yurchak Printing, Landisville, Pa.
Book printed and bound by Yurchak Printing, Landisville, Pa.
Date printed: May 2011
Printed in the United States of America

10 9 8 7 6 5 4 3 2 1

This book is printed on acid-free paper.

All links and Web addresses were checked and verified to be correct at the time of publication. Because of the dynamic nature of the Web, some addresses and links may have changed since publication and may no longer be valid.

Table of Contents

Introduction

Meteorology is the science of the atmosphere and its phenomena. When most people think of meteorologists, they think of their local television weatherperson who provides them with the daily forecast. But there are many other career options for meteorologists beyond broadcast meteorology. For example, there are meteorologists who create weather forecasts that keep us safe while flying; conduct research on global warming, pollution, and acid rain; and testify in legal proceedings about meteorological conditions that existed at the time of a crime or an accident. Other meteorologists work as storm spotters, tracking and studying tornadoes, hurricanes, and other severe weather in the field. Some people who are interested in meteorology work as college professors, writers and editors, scientific photographers, or consultants to politicians and private organizations that need expert information about meteorology. In short, there are career opportunities in meteorology for those with a variety of interests and skills.

Employment settings vary greatly for meteorologists. Some work in offices, classrooms, and in laboratories. Others work at weather stations. Although most of these weather stations are at airports located near cities, a number of weather stations are located in isolated and remote areas. One of the most remote meteorological posts is in the Antarctic. However, it provides some of the most interesting and relevant data in meteorology.

Meteorologists and support personnel are employed by state and federal agencies (such as the National Oceanic and Atmospheric Administration, National Science Foundation, National Aeronautics and Space Administration, Environmental Protection Agency, and the U.S. Departments of Agriculture, Defense, and Interior), colleges and universities, nonprofit organizations, and in private industry (by private weather consulting firms, engineering service firms, law firms, insurance companies, construction companies, large landscape businesses, utility companies, shipping companies, Internet weather providers, newspapers, recreational companies, commercial airlines, radio and television stations, and any other organization that needs weather forecasts or meteorological information).

Employment for atmospheric scientists (a career category that includes meteorologists) will grow faster than the average for all occupations through 2018, according to the U.S. Department of Labor. Opportunities will be best in private industry. Weather-sensitive industries like farming, commodity investments, utilities, transportation, and construction firms need more specific weather information than can be provided by the National Weather Service. They will require meteorologists to interpret the results of seasonal and other long-range forecasting research. The National Weather Service, a federal agency that employs a large number of meteorologists, has no plans to increase the number of weather stations or the number of meteorologists in existing stations for many years, and employment of meteorologists in other federal agencies is expected to remain stable.

Each article in *Careers in Focus: Meteorology* discusses a particular occupation in detail. Some of the articles appear in Ferguson's *Encyclopedia of Careers and Vocational Guidance*; others have been written especially for this book. Each article has been updated and revised with the latest information from the U.S. Department of Labor and other sources. Each article is broken down in the following manner.

The **Quick Facts** section provides a brief summary of the career, including recommended school subjects, personal skills, work environment, minimum educational requirements, salary ranges, certification or licensing requirements, and employment outlook. This section also provides acronyms and identification numbers for the following government classification indexes: the Dictionary of Occupational Titles (DOT), the Guide for Occupational Exploration (GOE), the National Occupational Classification (NOC) Index, and the Occupational Information Network (O*NET)-Standard Occupational Classification System (SOC) index. The DOT, GOE, and O*NET-SOC indexes have been created by the U.S. government; the NOC index is Canada's career classification system. Readers can use the identification numbers listed in the Quick Facts section to access further information about a career. Print editions of the DOT (*Dictionary of Occupational Titles*. Indianapolis, Ind.: JIST Works, 1991) and GOE (*Guide for Occupational Exploration*. Indianapolis, Ind.: JIST Works, 2001) are available at libraries. Electronic versions of the DOT (http://www.oalj.dol.gov/libdot.htm), NOC (http://www5.hrsdc.gc.ca/NOC), and O*NET-SOC (http://online.onetcenter.org) are available on the Internet. When no DOT, GOE, NOC, or O*NET-SOC numbers are listed, this means that the U.S. Department of Labor or Human Resources and Skills Development Canada have not created a numerical designation for this career. In this instance, you will see the acronym "N/A," or not available.

The **Overview** section is a brief introductory description of the duties and responsibilities involved in this career. Oftentimes, a career may have a variety of job titles. When this is the case, alternative career titles are presented. Employment statistics are also provided, when available. The **History** section describes the history of the particular job as it relates to the overall development of its industry or field. **The Job** describes the primary and secondary duties of the job. **Requirements** discusses high school and postsecondary education and training requirements, any certification or licensing that is necessary, and other personal requirements for success in the job. **Exploring** offers suggestions on how to gain experience in or knowledge of the particular job before making a firm educational and financial commitment. The focus is on what can be done while still in high school (or in the early years of college) to gain a better understanding of the job. The **Employers** section gives an overview of typical places of employment for the job. **Starting Out** discusses the best ways to land that first job, be it through the college career services office, newspaper ads, Internet employment sites, or personal contact. The **Advancement** section describes what kind of career path to expect from the job and how to get there. **Earnings** lists salary ranges and describes the typical fringe benefits. The **Work Environment** section describes the typical surroundings and conditions of employment—whether indoors or outdoors, noisy or quiet, social or independent. Also discussed are typical hours worked, any seasonal fluctuations, and the stresses and strains of the job. The **Outlook** section summarizes the job in terms of the general economy and industry projections. For the most part, Outlook information is obtained from the U.S. Bureau of Labor Statistics and is supplemented by information gathered from professional associations. Job growth terms follow those used in the *Occupational Outlook Handbook*. Growth described as "much faster than the average" means an increase of 20 percent or more. Growth described as "faster than the average" means an increase of 14 to 19 percent. Growth described as "about as fast as the average" means an increase of 7 to 13 percent. Growth described as "more slowly than the average" means an increase of 3 to 6 percent. "Little or no change" means a decrease of 2 percent to an increase of 2 percent. "Decline" means a decrease of 3 percent or more. Each article ends with **For More Information**, which lists organizations that provide information on training, education, internships, scholarships, and job placement.

Careers in Focus: Meteorology also includes photos, informative sidebars, and interviews with professionals in the field.

Aviation Meteorologists

QUICK FACTS

School Subjects
Earth science
Geography
Physics

Personal Skills
Helping/teaching
Technical/scientific

Work Environment
Primarily indoors
Primarily one location

Minimum Education Level
Bachelor's degree

Salary Range
$27,431 to $84,710 to
$127,250+

Certification or Licensing
Recommended

Outlook
About as fast as the average

DOT
025

GOE
02.01.01

NOC
2114

O*NET-SOC
19-2021.00

OVERVIEW

Aviation meteorologists conduct research and analyze data to provide forecasts of the weather conditions (wind speed, visibility, chance of rain, snow, etc.) for a given area. Their forecasts are used by the aviation community to improve the quality and safety of passenger and cargo flights and the efficiency of air navigation.

HISTORY

In 1927, Pan-Am was the first airline to hire a meteorology team. Within a decade, six other airlines joined suit. Northwest Airlines was the first to expand its meteorology team internationally, staffing offices on Shemya Island (a small island southwest of Alaska), Anchorage, Alaska; Seattle, Washington; New York, New York; Minneapolis-St. Paul, Minnesota; and in Tokyo, Japan.

By 1942, 17 airlines had dedicated meteorologists working on staff, but coming years would see those numbers fall. Today, commercial airlines and package delivery companies with meteorology departments include Delta, Southwest, FedEx, UPS, and Korean Air. Other airlines contract the work out to forecasting agencies.

Improved technology and methodologies have changed the work of aviation meteorologists from a reactive position to a proactive one. With new knowledge on how precipitation and wind currents can create turbulence that affect aircraft, they can better advise pilots on alternative routes rather than cancel flights outright.

Technology is also affecting the way meteorological information is shared internationally. In the early days, weather forecasts were hand-delivered to pilots or read via a radio transmission from the

A meteorologist (seated) at an aviation meteorology firm studies weather maps and discusses her findings with top executives. *(Ty Russell,* The Oklahoman/AP Photo)

flight deck. Now technological advances in sharing information is changing the landscape of aviation meteorology. With Internet broadcasting and stronger remote sensing equipment, fewer meteorologists and stations are required to cover an area. Additionally, airports now have Automated Weather Sensor Systems that relay information to flight towers around the world, making the sharing of weather information much more efficient.

Most recently in the news, a massive volcanic eruption in Iceland spewed ash thousands of feet into the air, creating a huge no-fly zone over much of Europe. The ash plume drifted at between 20,000 feet and 36,000 feet. There was a risk that that the ash could get sucked into airplane engines and cause them to shut down. The ash also affected visibility. Aviation meteorologists played a key role in advising air transportation officials regarding the dispersal of the ash and helped to determine when European skies were safe to fly again.

THE JOB

The weather we experience on the ground may be vastly different from the conditions at 30,000 feet above, the typical cruising altitude of a commercial jumbo jetliner, or at landing site. While it may be warm and sunny with clear skies at departure, pilots may encounter stormy conditions and turbulence once aloft, or conditions may be cold with low-lying fog at the flight's destination. It's no wonder then pilots are dependent on the work of aviation meteorologists to give them a better understanding of weather conditions during takeoffs, in flight, and during landings to ensure the safety of the aircraft and its passengers and crew.

Aviation meteorologists create forecasts using a variety of methods. They use information and images collected by satellites, model data from the National Centers for Environmental Prediction, or real-time data received from Doppler radar systems. Aviation meteorologists can also receive round-the-clock information from Automated Surface Observation System units that are located at all major airports in the United States. The Internet's technological advancements provide yet another source of information for aviation meteorologists. One example is the Collaborative Convective Forecast Product created by the Aviation Weather Center (AWC). This program allows meteorologists from different organizations, such as the Federal Aviation Administration, AWC, and private airlines, to make a combined forecast via the Internet. These combined forecasts provide up to a six-hour extended outlook for flight dispatchers to use in determining routes to pursue or those to avoid.

Aviation meteorologists watch for weather situations that may prove hazardous for flight navigation. Clouds, for example, may seem harmless to the average person, but can be quite dangerous if these cloud formations become unstable. Cloud formations known as cumulonimbus clouds can result in thunderstorms or turbulence.

The force of wind is another weather concern monitored by aviation meteorologists. When two wind forces move in opposite directions, they rub together creating a shear zone, or wind shear. This area is home to high degrees of turbulence, or whirling air masses. When detected, aviation meteorologists can immediately notify pilots flying into turbulence to prepare passengers for rough conditions or divert from their intended route.

Another example of an aviation-related weather issue is fog. Fog forms when the dew point and air temperature are only a few degrees from each other. While some patches of fog dissipate quickly, heavier fog, such as advection fog, can cause problems for pilots—especially when landing.

Aviation meteorologists consult Doppler radar for signs of precipitation. Airplanes still take off during periods of rain and snow; however flights may be delayed during periods of heavy precipitation. For example, aviation meteorologists can warn pilots of icing conditions—one of the more dangerous situations during flight travel. Icing—the formation of ice on part of the airplane—can cause braking systems to stall; the wings' slats, ailerons, and spoilers to stick; and hamper visibility on the cockpit windshield. Aviation meteorologists warn pilots of potential icing conditions and advise them to descend to a lower altitude and thus a warmer temperature, or they may advise flight dispatchers to delay takeoffs until these conditions improve.

Polar routes are being used more frequently by airlines as a way to reduce flight times and costs, especially for travel from Asia to North America. However, aviation meteorologists are faced with the difficulties of forecasting weather situations that are unique to this particular region. Besides conditions and altitudes prime for icing, aviation meteorologists must also keep track of space weather that may hamper a flight such as solar wind (which can create geomagnetic storms that can affect communications and power systems), solar radiation, and other issues associated with cross-polar traffic.

In addition to gathering data and creating forecasts, aviation meteorologists must be able to disseminate information as quickly and coherently as possible. They are in constant communication with pilots, airplane dispatchers, and air traffic controllers and provide up-to-the minute weather briefings.

Aerospace meteorologists are specialized meteorologists who prepare reports about weather conditions for spacecraft launches and landings. They make sure that weather conditions, both within our atmosphere and beyond, are safe for travel. These specialists have to account for temperature, wind, and visibility conditions that can delay or cancel a spacecraft launch or landing. Once the spacecraft is in orbit, aviation meteorologists study solar ray concentrations to be sure that radiation levels are safe for the craft and astronauts' exposure. They also must ensure that communication between ground control and the astronauts is not hampered by space weather. Aerospace meteorological weather services are provided by various government agencies and organizations, depending on the location of the spacecraft. Flight directors consult a combination of organizations such as the National Weather Service, private weather services, and meteorologists employed directly by NASA or the air force for their expertise.

REQUIREMENTS

High School

To prepare for a career as a meteorologist, take courses in mathematics (especially algebra, geometry, and trigonometry), earth science, geography, computer science, physics, and chemistry. A good command of English is essential because you must be able to describe complex weather events and patterns in a clear and concise way. Learning a foreign language, particularly Spanish, will also be of use as more airlines seek bilingual workers.

Postsecondary Training

You will need at least a bachelor's degree in meteorology to work as an aviation meteorologist. Some schools offer specializations or concentrations in aviation meteorology. The American Meteorological Society publishes a list of schools that offer degree programs in atmospheric and related sciences at its Web site, http://www.ametsoc.org/amsucar_curricula/index.cfm. Another list of education programs can be found at the National Weather Service's Web site, http://www.srh.noaa.gov/jetstream/nws/careers.htm.

For entry-level positions in the federal government, you must have a bachelor's degree (not necessarily in meteorology) with at least 24 semester hours of meteorology courses, including six hours in the analysis and prediction of weather systems and two hours of remote sensing of the atmosphere or instrumentation. Other required courses include calculus, physics, and other physical science courses, such as statistics, computer science, chemistry, physical oceanography, and physical climatology. You will need at least a master's degree in meteorology or a related area to work in research and teaching positions, as well as for other high-level positions in meteorology. Doctorates are quite common among high-level personnel.

Certification or Licensing

The American Meteorological Society confers the certified consulting meteorologist designation to meteorologists who meet educational requirements, have at least five years' experience in the field, meet character requirements, and pass an examination. Contact the society for more information.

Other Requirements

To be a successful meteorologist, you should be able to work well under pressure, have excellent communication skills, have a strong work ethic, be detail oriented, have knowledge of world geography, and be able to gather and study pertinent weather information quickly in order to pass it along to your employer in a prompt manner.

EXPLORING

One good way to learn more about careers in meteorology is to arrange for an information interview with a meteorologist who works at a local airport. Ask your high school counselor or a science teacher to help arrange this meeting. Contact meteorology associations for more information about the field. The American Meteorological Society, for example, offers a comprehensive career guide on its Web site, http://www.ametsoc.org/atmoscareers. Content includes suggestions on the types of course work and training to consider during the college years, various career opportunities, typical employers and workplaces, job and salary outlook statistics, and certification information. Read books about meteorology. Ask your school or community librarian to provide a few suggestions.

EMPLOYERS

Aviation meteorologists are employed by government agencies and the military (including the Department of Defense, the National Weather Service, the National Aeronautics and Space Administration, and the Federal Aviation Administration), and companies, such as airlines and private businesses that provide aviation meteorology consulting services to airlines, private aviation companies, and government agencies. Some aviation meteorologists teach at institutions of higher education.

STARTING OUT

There are several ways to enter the field of aviation meteorology. You can utilize the resources of your college's career services office to locate jobs or contact government agencies, airlines, and private consulting firms to investigate potential job openings. Additionally, the National Weather Association offers information on career paths for aviation meteorologists at its Web site, http://www.nwas.org.

ADVANCEMENT

Meteorologists employed by the National Weather Service and other government agencies advance according to civil service regulations. After meeting certain experience and education requirements, they advance to classifications that carry more pay and, often, more responsibility. Advancement opportunities available to meteorologists employed by airlines are more limited. A few of these workers, however, do advance to such positions as flight dispatcher and to administrative and supervisory positions. A few meteorologists go into business for themselves by establishing their own weather consulting services. Meteorologists who are employed in teaching and research in colleges and universities advance through academic promotions or by assuming administrative positions in the university setting.

EARNINGS

The U.S. Department of Labor reports that median annual earnings of atmospheric scientists were $84,710 in 2009. Salaries ranged from less than $40,560 to more than $127,250. The average salary for meteorologists employed by the federal government was $94,210.

Meteorologists with a bachelor of science degree are usually hired by the National Weather Service at the GS-5 to GS-7 grade levels; base salaries at these levels ranged from $27,431 (GS-5), to $30,577 (GS-6), to $33,979 (GS-7) in 2010. Those with a master of science degree enter at the GS-7 to GS-9 levels, which had base pay that ranged from $33,979 (GS-7), to $37,631 (GS-8), to $41,563 (GS-9). Meteorologists with Ph.D.'s enter at the GS-9 to GS-11 levels, which ranged from $41,563 (GS-9), to $45,771 (GS-10), to $50,287 (GS-11).

Benefits for aviation meteorologists depend on the employer; however, they usually include such items as health insurance, retirement or 401(k) plans, and paid vacation days.

WORK ENVIRONMENT

Aircraft fly 24 hours a day, seven days a week—which means that aviation meteorologists, often on a rotating basis, work evenings and weekends. The work environment can be demanding and stressful—especially when severe weather conditions exist. Despite the challenges of this career, aviation meteorologists take great pride in providing weather forecasts that help keep travelers safe and flight delays to a minimum. Meteorologists who work in college and university settings enjoy the same working conditions as other professors. They typically work nine months a year, with summers off for research or relaxation.

OUTLOOK

According to the *Occupational Outlook Handbook*, employment for meteorologists should grow faster than the average for all careers through 2018. While there will continue to be opportunities for aviation meteorologists, strong competition is expected for jobs since there is typically slow turnover in the field. Despite this prediction, the Federal Aviation Administration predicts that U.S. air traffic will double by 2025, and with weather cited as the cause of 70 percent of flight delays, aviation meteorologists will continue to be needed to prepare aviation forecasts and help airlines reduce delays. Overall, opportunities will be best for those with advanced degrees and certification.

FOR MORE INFORMATION

Visit the society's Web site for information on careers, certification, and membership and scholarships for college students; a searchable database of postsecondary training programs in meteorology; and answers to frequently asked questions about meteorology.
  American Meteorological Society
  45 Beacon Street
  Boston, MA 02108-3693
  Tel: 617-227-2425
  E-mail: amsinfo@ametsoc.org
  http://www.ametsoc.org

Fore information on aviation weather, contact the following organizations:
  Aviation Weather Center
  National Oceanic and Atmospheric Administration
  7220 NW 101st Terrace, Room 118
  Kansas City, MO 64153-2371
  http://aviationweather.gov

  Federal Aviation Administration
  800 Independence Avenue, SW
  Washington, DC 20591-0001
  Tel: 866-835-5322
  http://www.faa.gov

For information on industrial and applied meteorology, contact
  National Council of Industrial Meteorologists
  PO Box 721165
  Norman, OK 73070-4892
  Tel: 405-329-8707
  E-mail: info@ncim.org
  http://www.ncim.org

This government agency is concerned with describing and predicting changes in the environment, as well as managing marine and coastal resources. Visit its Web site for details on careers, summer programs and paid internships for young people, and financial aid for college-level students.

National Oceanic and Atmospheric Administration
1401 Constitution Avenue, NW, Room 5128
Washington, DC 20230-0001
http://www.noaa.gov

Visit the association's Web site for a list of schools with degree programs in meteorology or atmospheric science and information on scholarships and membership for college students.

National Weather Association
228 West Millbrook Road
Raleigh, NC 27609-4304
Tel: 919-845-7121
http://www.nwas.org

The NWS is an agency of the National Oceanic and Atmospheric Administration. Visit its Web site for comprehensive information on weather forecasting and weather phenomena.

National Weather Service (NWS)
1325 East West Highway
Silver Spring, MD 20910-3280
http://www.nws.noaa.gov

This United Nations agency focuses on meteorology (weather and climate), operational hydrology, and related geophysical sciences.

World Meteorological Organization
http://www.wmo.int/pages/index_en.html

INTERVIEW

Tim Burke has been an aviation meteorologist for 13 years. He discussed his career with the editors of Careers in Focus: Meteorology.

Q. What made you want to enter this career?

A. My interest in weather was mostly a hobby until 1994 when I decided to leave the insurance industry and return to school to earn a degree in meteorology. Honestly, I didn't intentionally become an aviation meteorologist—it happened more by luck. A position came open at American Airlines in Fort Worth,

Texas, as I was graduating. The position wasn't ideal since I was looking to find a position closer to my home near Chicago, but the flight benefits with American convinced me to take the job.

Q. What is one thing that young people may not know about a career in aviation meteorology?

A. Students considering a career in meteorology are lured to the major by the excitement of storm-chasing or being an on-air personality. Most students probably don't realize the amount of math and science prerequisites that are required within the major. Most of the major programs require four semesters of both physics and mathematics. Working as an aviation meteorologist requires shift work—with the likelihood of working nights, weekends, or holidays. You have to have a passion for weather or be a little crazy (maybe both) to seek this type of work.

Q. Can you please describe a day in your life on the job?

A. My job is to anticipate potential weather hazards, understand what impact these may have on the airlines' operations, prioritize the hazards, and then confidently communicate the information to the appropriate users. Each shift starts with a turnover briefing from the outgoing meteorologist. The details from this exchange serve as the starting point for a fresh data analysis to begin assembling the next set of forecasts. During this process there are scheduled briefings and ad hoc conferences. Ultimately the forecasts are issued and briefed. Once the forecast has been issued, the meteorologist focuses on monitoring the forecast and making changes as needed. Finally, the forecaster prepares for and conducts a briefing for the next shift. Usually there is time for lunch at your desk, but not always.

Q. What are the most important personal and professional qualities for aviation meteorologists?

A. First, you have to really enjoy the challenge of forecasting weather. Second, and probably the most difficult, is being able to admit that the forecast isn't working out and making a change. It's easy to misinterpret data, but it's important to learn from these situations and figure out what went wrong. A successful forecaster produces consistent forecasts, but also must be able to clearly communicate the same forecast to many different groups. Communication and confidence are huge—if the user doesn't trust you, then they won't advocate for your forecast. Aviation meteorologists must also be able prioritize, multitask, and meet deadlines.

Q. What are some of the pros and cons of your job?

A. There is rarely a dull day since there is almost always something significant weather-wise going on around the globe—even if it means alerting on a solar flare, volcanic eruption, or tsunami. Shifts fly by when there is a lot of weather to monitor and it's great to get paid for weather that I'd be monitoring at home anyway. There is a great deal of satisfaction making a great forecast and knowing that the customer used the information to make decisions that affect so many different people. Conversely, prolonged weather events can be mentally draining, and there are always those who will critique the forecast (including self-critique). Working holidays or weekends can be difficult when the rest of the world is relaxing or celebrating, but this is balanced by days off when everyone else is stuck in traffic or riding the train.

Q. What advice would you give to young people who are interested in meteorology? What is the employment outlook for aviation meteorologists?

A. Pursue your dream, but be prepared for hard work and realistic about future job opportunities. Choose a school that prepares you for the focus you have—whether that is broadcast, research, operational, etc. Consider a second major in computer science or business. Contact meteorologists to set up job shadows. Look for internships that will give you unique experience before you graduate—you need to stand out to get that job! Be willing to relocate to get that first job. Recent trends have been to outsource weather support and there is significant competition among private weather vendors resulting in lower entry-level salaries. Alternative energy companies have become a growth industry and an opportunity for meteorologists.

Broadcast Meteorologists

OVERVIEW

Broadcast meteorologists compile and analyze weather information and prepare reports for daily and nightly TV or radio newscasts. They create graphics, write scripts, and explain weather maps to audiences. Broadcast meteorologists, also known as *weathercasters*, also provide special reports during extreme weather conditions. To predict future weather patterns and to develop increased accuracy in weather study and forecasting, broadcast meteorologists may conduct research on such subjects as atmospheric electricity, clouds, precipitation, hurricanes, and data collected from weather satellites. Other areas of research used to forecast weather may include ocean currents and temperature.

HISTORY

Meteorology—the science that deals with the atmosphere and weather—is an observational science, involving the study of such factors as air pressure, climate, and wind velocity. Basic weather instruments were invented hundreds of years ago. Galileo invented the thermometer in 1593, and Evangelista Torricelli invented the barometer in 1643. Simultaneous comparison and study of weather in different areas was impossible until the telegraph was invented. Observations of the upper atmosphere from balloons and airplanes started after World War I. Not until World War II, however, was great financial support given to the

QUICK FACTS

School Subjects
Earth science
Physics
Speech

Personal Skills
Communication/ideas
Technical/scientific

Work Environment
Primarily indoors
Primarily one location

Minimum Education Level
Bachelor's degree

Salary Range
$19,650 to $85,760 to
$1,000,000+

Certification or Licensing
Recommended

Outlook
Decline

DOT
025

GOE
02.01.01

NOC
2114

O*NET-SOC
19-2021.00, 27-3022.00

Learn More About It

DiClaudio, Dennis. *Man vs. Weather: Be Your Own Weatherman.* New York: Penguin, 2008.

Dunlop, Storm. *The Weather Identification Handbook: The Ultimate Guide for Weather Watchers.* Guilford, Conn.: The Lyons Press, 2003.

Fine, Gary Alan. *Authors of the Storm: Meteorologists and the Culture of Prediction.* Chicago: University of Chicago Press, 2007.

Henson, Robert. *Weather on the Air: A History of Broadcast Meteorology.* Washington, D.C.: American Meteorological Society, 2010.

Smith, Mike. *Warnings: The True Story of How Science Tamed the Weather.* Austin, Tex.: Greenleaf Book Group Press, 2010.

development of meteorology. During this war a very clear-cut relationship was established between the effectiveness of new weapons and the atmosphere.

More accurate instruments for measuring and observing weather conditions, new systems of communication, and the development of satellites, radar, and high-speed computers to process and analyze weather data have helped broadcast meteorologists and the general public gain a better understanding of the atmosphere.

THE JOB

El Niño. F5-rated tornadoes storming down "tornado alley." Heat waves and ice storms. City-stopping 25-inch snowstorms. Flood-started fires in North Dakota. Hurricanes Katrina, Andrew, and Hugo. Extreme weather conditions often become national celebrities while the citizens of the threatened cities or regions suffer. These people look to broadcast meteorologists to advise them of upcoming storms, how to prepare for them, and how to recover from them. But broadcast meteorologists aren't just on the air during extreme conditions—they're on radio and TV broadcasts many times every day. On one day, people may rely on their local forecaster to alert them to the possibility of a tornado, on another day they may simply want to know whether to leave the house with an umbrella.

Some broadcast meteorologists are reporters with broadcasting degrees, but more than half of TV and radio weather forecasters have degrees in meteorology. Colleges across the country offer courses and degrees in meteorology for people who want to work for broadcast stations, weather services, research centers, flight centers, universities, and other places that study and record the weather. With a good background in the atmospheric sciences, broadcast meteorologists can make informed predictions about the weather and can clearly explain these predictions to the public.

Preparing a weather forecast means interpreting a great deal of data from a variety of different sources. The data may come from various weather stations around the world. Even the weather conditions swirling over the oceans can affect the weather of states far inland, so local weather forecasters keep track of the weather affecting distant cities. In addition, weather stations and ships at sea record atmospheric measurements, information that is then transmitted to other weather stations for analysis. This information makes its way to the National Weather Service, where scientists develop predictions to send to regional centers across the country. The tools used by meteorologists include weather balloons, instrumented aircraft, radar, satellites, and computers. Instrumented aircraft are high-performance airplanes used to observe many kinds of weather. Radar is used to detect rain or snow as well as other weather. Doppler radar can measure wind speed and direction. It has become the best tool for predicting severe weather. Satellites use advanced remote sensing technology to measure temperature, wind, and other characteristics of the atmosphere at many levels. Scientists can observe the entire surface of the earth with satellites. The introduction of computers has forever changed the research and forecasting of weather. The fastest computers are used in atmospheric research and for large-scale weather forecasting. Computers are used to produce simulations of upcoming weather.

Broadcast meteorologists may also prepare maps and graphics to aid the viewers. Broadcasting the information means reading and explaining the weather forecast to viewers and listeners. The broadcast weather forecaster must be able to concentrate on several different tasks at once. For example, when a forecaster broadcasts to the TV audience he or she is actually standing in front of a plain blue wall (called a "chromakey") that shows graphics only to the viewers. In order for the forecaster to see the map, he or she must watch the station's monitor. Then the broadcast meteorologist points to areas on the blue wall based on what he or she sees in the monitor; to the audience, it looks as though he or she is pointing to places on the map. While talking about the forecast, the broadcast meteorologist may have to listen to time cues (the amount of time left for the presentation) from the newscast producer through a hearing device placed in the ear. Throughout all this activity, the broadcast meteorologists must stay focused and calm.

Many people look to TV and radio news for weather information to help them plan events and vacations. Farmers are often able to protect their crops by following weather forecasts and advisories. The weather forecast is a staple element of most TV and radio newscasts. Some cable and radio stations broadcast weather reports 24 hours a day; most local network affiliates broadcast reports during morning, noon, and evening newscasts, as well as provide extended weather coverage during storms and other extreme conditions.

Broadcast meteorologists may also prepare weather forecasts and video and audio features for station Web sites. Some broadcast meteorologists also prepare weather pages for daily newspapers. For example, Tom Skilling, a well-known television weather forecaster for the WGN America cable network, also prepares a daily weather page for the *Chicago Tribune*.

In addition to broadcasting weather reports, radio and TV weather forecasters often visit schools and community centers to speak on weather safety. They are also frequently involved in broadcast station promotions, taking part in community events. Some broadcast meteorologists teach meteorology at colleges and universities.

REQUIREMENTS

High School

While you are in high school, you can prepare for a career as a broadcast meteorologist by taking a number of different classes. Concentrate on the sciences—earth science, biology, chemistry, and physics—to give you an understanding of the environment and how different elements interact. Geography and mathematics courses will also be useful to you. To familiarize yourself with computers and gain experience working with graphics programs, take computer classes. Computers will be an essential tool that you'll use throughout your career. Take plenty of English and speech classes. As a broadcaster, you will need to have excellent writing and speaking skills. If your school offers any media courses in which you learn how to broadcast a radio or television show, be sure to take these classes.

Postsecondary Training

Although a degree in meteorology or atmospheric science isn't required to enter the profession, it is necessary for advancement. The American Meteorological Society (AMS) publishes a list of schools that offer degree programs in atmospheric and related sciences at its Web site,

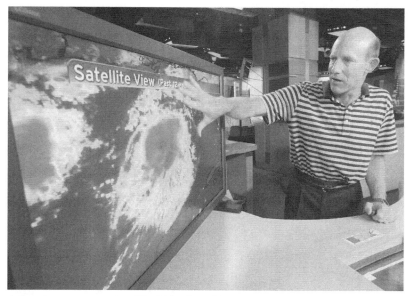

A hurricane expert for The Weather Channel discusses a satellite view of a tropical storm. *(Ric Feld, AP Photo)*

http://www.ametsoc.org/amsucar_curricula/index.cfm. Another list of education programs can be found at the National Weather Service's Web site, http://www.srh.noaa.gov/jetstream/nws/careers.htm. These programs typically include such courses as atmospheric measurements, thermodynamics and chemistry, radar, cloud dynamics, and physical climatology. While in college, you should also continue to take English, speech, and communications classes to hone your communication skills and computer classes to keep up to date with this technology. It is also important, during your college years, to complete an internship as a student weather forecaster with a TV or radio station. Your college and organizations such as the AMS can help you locate an internship. Visit http://www.ametsoc.org/amsstudentinfo/internships.html for a list of internship opportunities. Although it may not pay much—if anything—this position will allow you to make contacts with professionals and give you hands-on experience.

Certification or Licensing
The AMS and the National Weather Association (NWA) each offer certification to broadcast meteorologists. To qualify for the AMS Seal of Approval, you must meet educational requirements and demonstrate scientific competence and effective communication skills. You must submit recorded samples of your work for review by an

evaluation board. Requirements for the NWA Seal of Approval are similar, but you must also have a certain amount of on-air experience and pass a written exam. Although the AMS and the NWA seals are not required for broadcast meteorologists to work in this field, you will have an advantage when looking for a job if you hold these seals. Some TV and radio stations note that their forecaster has a seal of approval in their advertisements.

Other Requirements

As a broadcast meteorologist, you must be able to work well under pressure in order to meet deadlines for programming or plot severe weather systems. You must be able to communicate complex theories and events in a manner that is easy for the audience to understand. You should have a strong speaking voice and clear enunciation. And, naturally, you must have an interest in weather and the environment.

EXPLORING

There are several ways you can explore different aspects of this career while you are still in school. Consider joining a science club that is involved in environmental activities. Ask a teacher or school counselor to schedule a trip to a local television station so you can see firsthand what this work environment is like. It is also a good idea to volunteer to work at your school's radio or TV station. You'll learn the basics of putting on a program and might even get on the air yourself. If your school doesn't have one of these stations, join the newspaper staff to get some experience working with the media. In addition, pay attention to the weathercasters on your local news and on The Weather Channel (http://www.weather.com) to become familiar with how to deliver your forecasts.

Each year, the National Weather Service (NWS) accepts a limited number of student volunteers, mostly college students but also a few high school students. Local offices of the NWS also allow the public to come in for tours by appointment. Your counselor may be able to help you with this.

Also, contact your local radio and TV stations and ask for a tour. Tell them you are interested in broadcast meteorology and ask to meet the weather forecasting staff. You may be able to arrange for an information interview with a broadcast meteorologist, during which you might ask that person about his or her education, experiences, the best part of the work, and any other questions you may have.

EMPLOYERS

Most broadcast meteorologists work for network television affiliates and local radio stations. Because evening national newscasts do not have weather forecasts, there are fewer network opportunities for broadcast meteorologists. National cable networks, such as The Weather Channel and 24-hour news channels, hire weather forecasters and may offer internships.

Those who have degrees in meteorology or atmospheric science can work for a variety of other services as well—the U.S. government is the largest employer of meteorologists in the country. Meteorologists work for the NWS, the military, the Department of Agriculture, NASA, and other agencies.

STARTING OUT

Your college's career services office is a good resource to use when you are looking for your first job. Many people also find their first positions either through connections they have made while interning or through the internship itself.

Local ads and job listings on the Internet are other sources you should check out. The American Meteorological Society, the National Weather Association, and various broadcast media associations provide job listings at their Web sites.

ADVANCEMENT

Someone forecasting for a network affiliate in a smaller region may want to move to a larger city and a larger audience. In many cases, meteorologists work up within one station. Full-time broadcast meteorologists generally start forecasting for the weekend news or the morning news, then move up to the evening news. A meteorologist may then become *chief meteorologist*, in charge of a newscast's weather center and staff. With each advancement comes more responsibility and a larger salary.

EARNINGS

In the newsroom, broadcast meteorologists generally make more than sportscasters but less than lead anchors. The salary for weather forecasters varies greatly according to experience, region, and media. Those working in television typically earn more than those working in radio. Broadcast meteorologists earned mean annual salaries of

$85,760 in 2009, according to the U.S. Department of Labor (DOL). Broadcast meteorologists at radio stations in small markets may earn less than $19,650 a year, while well-known television meteorologists in large markets such as Chicago or New York may earn more than $1 million a year.

Employers offer a variety of benefit packages, which can include any of the following: paid holidays, vacations, and sick days; personal days; medical, dental, and life insurance; profit-sharing plans; 401(k) plans; retirement and pension plans; and educational assistance programs.

WORK ENVIRONMENT

The atmosphere at a radio or TV station can be exciting, fun, and sometimes tense—especially during times of emergency. Forecasters' schedules depend on the times they are scheduled to be on the air. Those working morning shows, for example, may have to be at the station by 4 A.M. to prepare for the broadcast. The weather forecaster may also make public appearances, giving talks to schools or clubs. This gives the forecaster the opportunity to meet a lot of people and attend events; however, it also makes for busy and varied days. In addition, they have to be prepared to work odd or long hours during times of weather emergencies.

Broadcast meteorologists work with a great deal of specialized equipment, such as computers and radar, as well as the equipment of the broadcast trade, such as the chromakey, hearing devices, and microphones. The weather forecaster is part of a team (along with such professionals as newscasters, producers, and technicians) who work to put the broadcast on the air.

OUTLOOK

The DOL predicts that employment for all atmospheric scientists will increase faster than the average for all careers through 2018. However, it also predicts that employment for television and radio announcers will decline slowly throughout the same time period. Usually, meteorologists are able to find work in the field upon graduation, though they may have to be flexible about the area of meteorology and region of the country in which they work. Positions for broadcast meteorologists, as with any positions in broadcast news, are in high demand. The growing number of graduates looking for work in news departments will keep the field very competitive.

Currently more than half of TV and radio weather forecasters hold meteorology degrees; with increased competition for work, forecasters without extensive educational backgrounds in the atmospheric sciences may find it difficult to get jobs. New tools and computer programs for the compilation and analyses of data are constantly being developed by research scientists. To find good positions, future broadcast meteorologists will need a lot of technical expertise in addition to their understanding of weather.

A national fascination with weather may lead to more outlets for broadcast meteorologists. Look for more cable weather information channels like The Weather Channel to develop. Weather disasters are requiring more coverage by news departments. In addition to forecasting, broadcast meteorologists will be involved in reporting about the after-effects of storms and other extreme conditions. Broadcast meteorologists are also becoming more actively involved in developing and maintaining pages on the Internet and using social media to communicate with the public.

FOR MORE INFORMATION

Contact the alliance for information on careers in radio and television, as well as scholarships and internships for college students.
Alliance for Women in Media
1760 Old Meadow Road, Suite 500
McLean, VA 22102-4306
Tel: 703-506-3290
http://www.awrt.org

For information on union membership, contact
American Federation of Radio and Television Artists
260 Madison Avenue
New York, NY 10016-2401
Tel: 212-532-0800
http://www.aftra.org

Visit the society's Web site for information on careers, certification, and membership and scholarships for college students; a searchable database of postsecondary training programs in meteorology; and answers to frequently asked questions about meteorology.
American Meteorological Society
45 Beacon Street
Boston, MA 02108-3693
Tel: 617-227-2425
E-mail: amsinfo@ametsoc.org
http://www.ametsoc.org

*An association of university broadcasting faculty, industry profes-
sionals, and graduate students, BEA offers annual scholarships in
broadcasting for college juniors, seniors, and graduate students.
Visit its Web site for useful information about broadcast education
and the broadcasting industry.*

Broadcast Education Association (BEA)
1771 N Street, NW
Washington, DC 20036-2891
Tel: 202-429-3935
http://www.beaweb.org

Contact the association for information on union membership.

National Association of Broadcast Employees and Technicians
501 Third Street, NW
Washington, DC 20001-2760
http://nabetcwa.org

*The association provides information on broadcast education,
scholarships for college students, jobs, and useful publications at
its Web site.*

National Association of Broadcasters
1771 N Street, NW
Washington, DC 20036-2800
Tel: 202-429-5300
E-mail: nab@nab.org
http://www.nab.org

*This government agency is concerned with describing and predict-
ing changes in the environment, as well as managing marine and
coastal resources. Visit its Web site for details on careers, summer
programs and paid internships for young people, and financial aid
for college-level students.*

National Oceanic and Atmospheric Administration
1401 Constitution Avenue, NW, Room 5128
Washington, DC 20230-0001
http://www.noaa.gov

*Visit the association's Web site for a list of schools with degree pro-
grams in meteorology or atmospheric science and information on
scholarships and membership for college students.*

National Weather Association
228 West Millbrook Road
Raleigh, NC 27609-4304

Tel: 919-845-7121
http://www.nwas.org

The NWS is an agency of the National Oceanic and Atmospheric Administration. Visit its Web site for comprehensive information on weather forecasting and weather phenomena.
National Weather Service (NWS)
1325 East West Highway
Silver Spring, MD 20910-3280
http://www.nws.noaa.gov

This United Nations agency focuses on meteorology (weather and climate), operational hydrology, and related geophysical sciences.
World Meteorological Organization
http://www.wmo.int/pages/index_en.html

Climatologists

QUICK FACTS

School Subjects
Earth science
Geography
Physics

Personal Skills
Helping/teaching
Technical/scientific

Work Environment
Indoors and outdoors
One location with some
  travel

Minimum Education Level
Bachelor's degree

Salary Range
$27,431 to $84,710 to
  $127,250+

Certification or Licensing
Recommended

Outlook
Faster than the average

DOT
025

GOE
02.01.01

NOC
2114

O*NET-SOC
19-2021.00, 19-2041.01

OVERVIEW

Climatologists study past weather data to determine weather patterns and trends for a given region. They compile, conduct statistical analyses of, and interpret data on temperature, sunlight, rainfall, humidity, and wind for a particular area over months, years, or centuries for use in weather forecasting and aviation, historical research, agriculture, commerce, and public health planning.

HISTORY

The medieval Chinese scientist Shen Kuo can be considered one of the earliest known climatologists. After discovering petrified bamboo underground in a dry climate area unsuitable for the growth of bamboo, Shen Kuo deduced that climates naturally shifted over an enormous span of time.

Other early climate researchers include Edmund Halley, for whom the famous comet is named after, who published a map of the trade winds in 1686. Halley identified solar heating as the cause of atmospheric changes. Benjamin Franklin can be considered another early climatologist. In the 18th century, he was the first to map the course of the Gulf Stream for use in sending mail from the United States to countries overseas. Through the first half of the 20th century, the prevailing view saw climate as a static condition. The study of climate change (what to many scientists seemed a contradiction in terms) was only an occasional interest of individuals who worked in different scientific fields.

One immense climate change that encouraged the study of climatology was ice ages. Milutin Milankovitch was best known for his theory on ice ages, relating these changes to the variations of the earth's orbit. These long-term climate changes are now known as Milankovitch cycles

The Second World War encouraged a rapid growth of meteorology and geophysics. Helmut Landsberg's 1941 textbook *Physical Climatology* illustrated how physical principles can explain the general features of global climate and promoted climatology as a truly scientific field. Landsberg's statistical analyses aided military operations during the war.

Up until the 1960s, there had never been a community of people studying long-term climate change. It was at this time that scientists, concerned about global warming, worked to get governmental and international agencies to organize their diverse research efforts through central offices and committees.

Weather Extremes: Highest Temperatures Recorded on Earth by Continent

Continent	Location	Temperature (in Fahrenheit)	Date
1. Africa	El Azizia, Libya	136 degrees	September 13, 1922
2. North America	Death Valley, United States	134 degrees	July 10, 1913
3. Asia	Tirat Tsvi, Israel (present-day)	129 degrees	June 22, 1942
4. Australia	Cloncurry	128 degrees	January 16, 1889
5. Europe	Seville, Spain	122 degrees	August 4, 1881
6. South America	Rivadavia, Argentina	120 degrees	December 11, 1905
7. Oceania	Tuguegarao, Philippines	108 degrees	April 29, 1912
8. Antarctica	Vanda Station, Scott Coast	59 degrees	January 5, 1974

Source: National Climatic Data Center

By the end of the century, the study of climatology emerged as a distinct practice area. Scientists who once might have called themselves oceanographers or meteorologists were now designated "climate scientists" or "climatologists."

Most recently, the Intergovernmental Panel on Climate Change (IPCC) was created to bring together a community of experts on the causes of global warming. This panel, which meets every decade or so, has grown to include more than 150 published researchers, plus some 600 reviewers. The IPCC demonstrates the growth and dependence on this specialized scientific community on which the world's policymakers now rely on for crucial advice regarding climate change.

THE JOB

Climatologists study long-term weather data and patterns—ranging from months, to years, to centuries ago—to help predict climate changes and their effect on the environment (including plants and animals), energy usage, food production, and human health and life expectancy. With their background in math, physical science, and biological science, and training in meteorology, climatologists are responsible for collecting, analyzing, researching, and reporting on the climate on a local, regional, or global level. Although they often have educational backgrounds in meteorology, they differ greatly from traditional meteorologists who focus on and predict short-term weather changes.

Climatologists use a variety of information sources, investigative techniques, and tools, depending on the scope of the region they study, the goal of their research, and their employer. They may interpret data regarding wind, rainfall, sunlight, or temperature from meteorological stations, Doppler radar stations, or images from satellites. They may also rely on the information provided by computer models. They also might study the fossil record, tree rings, and geological formations to learn about past climates. Oftentimes they consult with other climatologists, meteorologists, and other scientists.

Climatologists also realize the importance of climate models in understanding the dynamics and future projections of weather. For example, they may consider the El Niño-Southern Oscillation (ENSO) phenomenon in their work. ENSO, because of its temperature fluctuation in the eastern portion of the Pacific Ocean, has a profound effect on the climate of the tropics and subtropics, as well as other regions. From past records, climatologists know that during an ENSO occurrence—this cycle occurs every two to seven years—certain weather patterns will emerge. Heavy rains will fall in certain places located around the Pacific, Atlantic, and Indian Oceans, but not in other areas. This disparity is a huge factor for drought (a period of extremely low or no rainfall). Climatologists can predict the occurrence of an ENSO by using tools and methods such as computer models and moored, drifting, or expendable buoys. Their ENSO predictions can help countries, especially those dependent on the oceans for their economic livelihood, better prepare for extreme climate episodes. On the other hand, when predictions are positive, farmers, fishermen, and foresters can plan accordingly to take economic advantage of favorable weather conditions.

Other industries rely on the research of climatologists to help them in their work. When building a new structure in an arid area such as southern Arizona, engineers may consult with climatologists and use their long-term climate predictions to create better designs for heating and cooling systems.

Climatologists not only study local and regional climates, as well as climate on a global scale, they also study how human-induced factors play a role in causing climates to change. For example, climatologists monitor the atmospheric aerosol content—the microscopic particles in the atmosphere. While some of these particles occur naturally, the majority are human-made—composed of mineral dust, carbon or soot emissions, or ammonium sulfate. Climatologists' interpretations of these levels are used by environmentalists to warn the public about the negative long-term effects of emissions: a gradual global warming that may be disastrous to the earth and its inhabitants.

Some climatologists may specialize in a particular region or weather pattern. *Mesoscale climatologists* specialize in studying storm systems or storm patterns such as tornadoes, often focusing on a particular region. Those studying large-scale weather patterns such as Asian monsoons or the El Niño effect are called *synoptic-scale climatologists*. *Economic meteorologists* are climatologists who are interested in how the weather plays a role in issues ranging from agricultural production to the economic effects of global warming.

According to the American Association of State Climatologists, 47 states and Puerto Rico have an official state climatologist who is responsible for providing climate services for their state and the nation as a whole. They are either employees of a state agency or on the staff of a state-funded university. These state climatologists are recognized by the National Climatic Data Center of the National Oceanic and Atmospheric Administration.

REQUIREMENTS

High School
To prepare for a career as a climatologist, take classes in mathematics, biology, physics, earth science, computer science, economics, and chemistry. English and speech classes will help you develop your oral and written communication skills.

Postsecondary Training
To become a climatologist, you will need to earn at least a bachelor's degree in climatology, meteorology, or another atmospheric science;

Weather Extremes: Lowest Temperatures Recorded on Earth by Continent

Continent	Location	Temperature (in Fahrenheit)	Date
1. Antarctica	Vostok	–129 degrees	July 21, 1983
2. Asia (tie)	Oimekon, Russia	–90 degrees	February 6, 1933
	Verkhoyansk, Russia	–90 degrees	February 7, 1982
3. Greenland	Northice	–87 degrees	January 9, 1954
4. North America	Snag, Yukon, Canada	–81.4 degrees	February 3, 1947
5. Europe	Ust'Shchugor, Russia	–67 degrees	unavailable
6. South America	Sarmiento, Argentina	–27 degrees	June 1, 1907
7. Africa	Ifrane, Morocco	–11 degrees	February 11, 1935
8. Australia	Charlotte Pass	–9.4 degrees	June 29, 1994
9. Oceania	Mauna Kea Observatory, United States	12 degrees	May 17, 1979

Source: National Climatic Data Center

University of Florida climatologists discuss the possible agricultural effects of a recently developed El Niño weather event. Caused by warmer-than-average surface waters in the Pacific Ocean, El Niño brings increased rainfall and cool temperatures to the Southeast during winter and spring. *(Josh Wickham, University of Florida/IFAS/AP Photo)*

earth science; or a related field of study. In college, you will take courses such as calculus, physics, and other physical science courses, such as statistics, computer science, geology, chemistry, physical oceanography, and physical climatology. If you are interested in pursuing teaching and research positions, you will need at least a master's degree. Doctorates are required for top research and academic positions.

Certification or Licensing

The American Meteorological Society confers the certified consulting meteorologist designation to meteorologists who meet educational requirements, have at least five years' experience in the field, meet character requirements, and pass an examination. Contact the society for more information on certification requirements.

Other Requirements

To be a successful climatologist, you should be curious and like to solve problems. You should also be detail oriented and enjoy conducting methodical research. Other important traits for climatologists include a willingness to travel to conduct research, strong communication skills, and the ability to work well with others.

EXPLORING

There are many ways to learn more about careers in climatology. You can read books about the field such as *Understanding Weather and Climate*, 5th edition, by Edward Aguado and James E. Burt (Upper Saddle River, N.J.: Prentice Hall, 2009), and *Meteorology Today: An Introduction to Weather, Climate, and the Environment*, 9th edition, by C. Donald Ahrens (Florence, Ky.: Brooks Cole, 2008). You can also check out Web sites such as Climatology News (http://www.climatologynews.com) for more information about the field. Other good ways to learn more about the field include talking to a climatologist about his or her career or contacting meteorology associations. The American Meteorological Society, for example, offers a comprehensive career guide on its Web site, http://www.ametsoc.org/atmoscareers. Content includes suggestions on the types of course work and training to consider during the college years, various career opportunities, typical employers and workplaces, job and salary outlook statistics, and certification information.

EMPLOYERS

Climatologists are employed by state and federal government agencies (such as the National Oceanic and Atmospheric Administration and the U.S. Department of Agriculture), private companies that provide climatological analyses for industry or government agencies, and colleges and universities. Some climatologists work as freelance consultants.

STARTING OUT

Many climatologists land their first jobs as a result of contacts made during internships or fellowships with government agencies or private research organizations. Job leads can also be found via college career services offices, professional associations, and by direct application to government agencies and private companies that employ climatologists.

ADVANCEMENT

Climatologists who are employed by government agencies advance according to civil service regulations. They receive higher pay and managerial responsibilities. Those who work for private research organizations and companies advance by receiving pay raises, managerial duties, and more prestigious research assignments. The normal pattern of advancement for college professors is from instructor to assistant professor, to associate professor, to full professor.

EARNINGS

The median annual earnings of atmospheric scientists (including climatologists) were $84,710 in 2009, according to the U.S. Department of Labor. Those just starting out in the field earned less than $40,560, while very experienced workers earned more than $127,250. The average salary for atmospheric scientists who worked for the federal government was $94,210 in 2009, while those employed by colleges and universities earned $80,870 a year.

Atmospheric scientists with a bachelor of science degree are usually hired by the National Weather Service at the GS-5 to GS-7 grade levels; base salaries at these levels ranged from $27,431 (GS-5), to $30,577 (GS-6), to $33,979 (GS-7) in 2010. Those with a master of science degree enter at the GS-7 to GS-9 levels, which had base pay that ranged from $33,979 (GS-7), to $37,631 (GS-8), to $41,563 (GS-9). Meteorologists with Ph.D.'s enter at the GS-9 to GS-11 levels, which ranged from $41,563 (GS-9), to $45,771 (GS-10), to $50,287 (GS-11).

Benefits for meteorologists depend on the employer; however, they usually include such items as health insurance, retirement or 401(k) plans, and paid vacation days.

WORK ENVIRONMENT

Work environments for climatologists vary greatly by position. Some climatologists spend all or much of their time in offices or laboratories. Others spend most of their working hours in the field conducting research in a variety of climates and weather conditions. Field research may be conducted in the Arctic, in deserts, at the bottom of the ocean in a submersible, or at the top of a 10,000-foot-tall mountain. Climatologists who participate in field research must be prepared to spend weeks and even months away from friends and family. College teachers enjoy comfortable work settings and work nine months a year, with summers free for research or relaxation.

OUTLOOK

Employment for atmospheric scientists should grow faster than the average for all careers through 2018, according to the *Occupational Outlook Handbook*. There should be strong demand for climatologists to study the historical meteorological record and help develop action plans to fight global warming and address other weather-related challenges. Although employment is expected to be good, there will be strong competition for jobs. Opportunities will be best for climatologists with certification and advanced degrees.

FOR MORE INFORMATION

For information on the career of state climatologist, contact
American Association of State Climatologists
http://www.stateclimate.org

Visit the society's Web site for information on careers, certification, and membership and scholarships for college students; a searchable database of postsecondary training programs in meteorology; and answers to frequently asked questions about meteorology.
American Meteorological Society
45 Beacon Street
Boston, MA 02108-3693
Tel: 617-227-2425
E-mail: amsinfo@ametsoc.org
http://www.ametsoc.org

Contact the following National Oceanic and Atmospheric Administration organizations for more information about climatology and climate statistics:

Climate Prediction Center
5200 Auth Road
Camp Springs, MD 20746-4325
http://www.cpc.ncep.noaa.gov

National Climatic Data Center
Federal Building
151 Patton Avenue
Asheville NC 28801-5001
Tel: 828-271-4800
http://www.ncdc.noaa.gov/oa/ncdc.html

For information on industrial and applied meteorology, contact
National Council of Industrial Meteorologists
PO Box 721165
Norman, OK 73070-4892
Tel: 405-329-8707
E-mail: info@ncim.org
http://www.ncim.org

The National Oceanic and Atmospheric Administration says that its reach "goes from the surface of the sun to the depths of the ocean floor." Visit its Web site for information on careers, summer programs and paid internships for young people, and financial aid for college-level students.

National Oceanic and Atmospheric Administration
1401 Constitution Avenue, NW, Room 5128
Washington, DC 20230-0001
http://www.noaa.gov

Visit the association's Web site for a list of schools with degree programs in meteorology or atmospheric science and information on scholarships and membership for college students.

National Weather Association
228 West Millbrook Road
Raleigh, NC 27609-4304
Tel: 919-845-7121
http://www.nwas.org

The NWS is an agency of the National Oceanic and Atmospheric Administration. Visit its Web site for information on weather forecasting and weather phenomena.
National Weather Service (NWS)
1325 East West Highway
Silver Spring, MD 20910-3280
http://www.nws.noaa.gov

This United Nations agency focuses on meteorology (weather and climate), operational hydrology, and related geophysical sciences.
World Meteorological Organization
http://www.wmo.int/pages/index_en.html

INTERVIEW

Mary Stampone is the state climatologist for New Hampshire and an assistant professor of geography in the Department of Geography at the University of New Hampshire. She discussed her career with the editors of Careers in Focus: Meteorology.

Q. How long have you worked in the field?

A. I have been a professional in the field for two years but have been studying climatology through graduate work for 12 years.

Q. What made you want to enter this career?

A. I originally began my studies in earth sciences as a geology major in college. This was during the late 1990s when reports on the human impact, particularly greenhouse gases, on climate were becoming a big part of the public conversation. I started getting interested in the interactions between processes at the earth's surface, both natural and anthropogenic, and the atmosphere above and decided to pursue graduate work in the area of climate system science.

Q. Can you tell us about the New Hampshire State Climate Office (NHSCO) and your position as New Hampshire state climatologist? Describe a day in your life on the job.

A. The NHSCO is one of many state climate offices, each of which varies depending on the needs of the state in which they are located. The NHSCO is located within the Department of Geography, College of Liberal Arts, at the University of New Hampshire (UNH)—a land, sea, and space grant institution.

The NHSCO maintains climate and weather records for the state of New Hampshire and serves as a point of contact for government agencies engaged in climate monitoring activities within the state and serves as scientific resource on climate for the citizens of New Hampshire.

In addition to being the state climatologist, I am a faculty member in the Department of Geography at the UNH. Therefore my days focus on my faculty duties and the time I spend on NHSCO activities vary as needed. Days when significant weather is happening in the state will include interviews with local media outlets. I also respond to citizen requests for weather and climate data and present to schools, discussion groups, businesses, and other organizations. I maintain weather stations near campus and collect weather data daily. I also research climate issues that are of interest to New Hampshire citizens.

Other state climate offices operate differently depending on the needs of the citizens and the organizations that sponsor them.

Q. What is one thing that young people may not know about a career in climatology?

A. It is a quantitative, scientific discipline that requires a solid background in math and science. Students interested in pursuing a career in climatology will need to take course work in calculus, statistics, and physics in addition to classes focusing on the study of climate.

Q. What are the most important personal and professional qualities for climatologists?

A. As with any discipline, being thorough and objective researchers is of the utmost importance. Climatology has broader implications for numerous disciplines and the study of climate is interdisciplinary by nature. It is therefore important to be able to work with others across disciplines. Climate data and information are also important for those outside the research community, and there are a variety of users at all levels of familiarity with climate data and information. Therefore it is also important to be able to communicate complex research methods and outcomes to a variety of people from different academic disciplines as well as those outside the academic and research community.

Q. What are some of the pros and cons of your job?

A. Being able to study the natural world in which we live and being able to communicate that information to the scientific community and a public eager to know more about an issue that affects their lives is incredibly rewarding. As with research in any discipline, climate research is time consuming and the work can be tedious, but the process of discovery and adding to our understanding about the world around us is the best part of the job.

Q. What advice would you give to young people who are interested in the field?

A. Prepare yourself academically by taking course work in math and science but also take time to observe the weather and read about and discuss issues in climate science. Be involved in climate and weather monitoring either through climate monitoring programs, like CoCoRaHS (http://www.cocorahs.org), on your own by purchasing or building your own weather station, or by simply taking the time to look around.

College Professors, Meteorology/ Atmospheric Science

OVERVIEW

College meteorology/atmospheric science professors instruct undergraduate and graduate students about these fields and related subjects at colleges and universities. They lecture classes, supervise labs, and create and grade examinations. They also may conduct field research, write for publication, and aid in administration. Approximately 9,900 postsecondary atmospheric, earth, marine, and space sciences teachers are employed in the United States.

HISTORY

The concept of colleges and universities goes back many centuries. These institutions evolved slowly from monastery schools, which trained a select few for certain professions, notably theology. The terms *college* and *university* have become virtually interchangeable in America outside the walls of academia, although originally they designated two very different kinds of institutions.

Two of the most notable early European universities were the University of Bologna in Italy and the University of Paris. The University of Bologna was thought to have been established in the 12th century and the University of Paris was chartered in 1201. These universities were considered to be models after which other European universities were

QUICK FACTS

School Subjects
Biology
Earth science
Physics
Speech

Personal Skills
Communication/ideas
Helping/teaching
Technical/scientific

Work Environment
Indoors and outdoors
One location with some travel

Minimum Education Level
Master's degree

Salary Range
$43,350 to $78,660 to $133,080+

Certification or Licensing
None available

Outlook
Faster than the average

DOT
025, 090

GOE
02.01.01, 12.03.02

NOC
2114, 4121

O*NET-SOC
19-2021.00, 25-1051.00

patterned. Oxford University in England was probably established during the 12th century. Oxford served as a model for early American colleges and universities and today is still considered one of the world's leading institutions.

Harvard, the first U.S. college, was established in 1636. Its stated purpose was to train men for the ministry. All of the early colleges were

SOARS

SOARS, which stands for Significant Opportunities in Atmospheric Research and Science, is a unique summer internship program for scientific-minded college students that combines hands-on research with focused mentoring. Participants spend 10 weeks conducting research and meeting with scientists in their chosen interest to formulate a scientific paper to present at a closing colloquium. Sound intimidating? With up to five mentors assigned per participant, each SOAR "protégé" is well supported throughout his or her internship.

Examples of topics from previous colloquiums include:

- Assessing tropical cyclone contribution to annual global rainfall
- The effects of differential rotation on one to two solar mass stars
- Impacts of climate change on the summer rainfall of the southern Rocky Mountains

Students are encouraged to participate each summer of their college experience to provide valuable experience, connections, and skills—all useful assets when applying for a graduate program.

Students from many educational backgrounds—such as meteorology, chemistry, physics, engineering, mathematics, ecology, and the social sciences—are encouraged to apply. Also encouraged are students from groups historically underrepresented in the sciences, including African American, American Indian or Alaska Native, Hispanic or Latino, female, first-generation college students, and students with disabilities.

SOARS protégés stay at furnished accommodations at no added cost and receive a competitive stipend for their work performed during the internship. The program typically runs from the end of May to August, and the deadline for application is in February. Visit http://www.soars.ucar.edu for complete details and an online application.

established for religious training. With the growth of state-supported institutions in the early 18th century, the process of freeing the curriculum from ties with the church began. The University of Virginia established the first liberal arts curriculum in 1825, and these innovations were later adopted by many other colleges and universities.

Although the original colleges in the United States were patterned after Oxford University, they later came under the influence of German universities. During the 19th century, more than 9,000 Americans went to Germany to study. The emphasis in German universities was on the scientific method. Most of the people who had studied in Germany returned to the United States to teach in universities, bringing this objective, factual approach to education, the sciences (including chemistry, biology, and mathematics), and other fields of learning.

People have studied weather phenomena since ancient times, but formal educational training in meteorology did not become available until recent times. Today, meteorology and other atmospheric science programs are increasingly being offered at U.S. colleges and universities. In fact, there are now more than 100 undergraduate and graduate atmospheric science programs in the United States, according to the American Meteorological Society (AMS).

THE JOB

College and university faculty members teach meteorology, atmospheric science, or related subjects at junior colleges or at four-year colleges and universities. At four-year institutions, most faculty members are *assistant professors, associate professors*, or *full professors*. These three types of professorships differ in regards to status, job responsibilities, and salary. Assistant professors are new faculty members who are working to get tenure (status as a permanent professor); they seek to advance to associate and then to full professorships.

College meteorology/atmospheric science professors perform three main functions: teaching, service, and research. Their most important responsibility is to teach students. Their role within the department will determine the level of courses they teach and the number of courses per semester. Most professors work with students at all levels, from college freshmen to graduate students. They may teach several classes a semester or only a few each year. Though professors may spend only 12 to 16 hours a week in the actual classroom, they spend many hours preparing lesson plans, grading assignments and exams, and preparing grade reports. They also schedule office or computer laboratory hours during the week to be available to students outside of regular classes, and they meet with students individually throughout the semester. Many professors also work in the field as practicing meteorologists and atmospheric scientists.

In the classroom, meteorology/atmospheric science professors teach a variety of classes such as Introduction to Meteorology, Synoptic Meteorology, Weather Forecasting, Physical Meteorology, Dynamic Meteorology, Environmental Climatology and Laboratory, Computational Methods in the Field Sciences, Hydrology, Thermodynamics and the Boundary Layer, Atmospheric Sensing Methods, Air Pollution Meteorology, and Tropical Meteorology.

In addition to teaching classes, professors also administer exams and assign textbook reading and other research. In some courses, professors rely heavily on laboratories to transmit course material.

An important part of teaching is advising students. Not all meteorology/atmospheric science professors serve as advisers, but those who do must set aside large blocks of time to guide students through the program. College professors who serve as advisers may have any number of students assigned to them, from fewer than 10 to more than 100, depending on the administrative policies of the college. Their responsibility may involve looking over a planned program of studies to make sure the students meet requirements for graduation, or it may involve working intensively with each student on many aspects of college life. They may also discuss the different fields of meteorology and atmospheric science with students and help them identify potential career paths.

All college professors provide important services to their department, college, or profession. Many college professors edit technical journals, review research and scholarship, and head committees about their field of expertise. College professors also serve on committees that determine the curriculum or make decisions about student learning.

The third responsibility of meteorology/atmospheric science professors is research and publication. Faculty members who are heavily involved in research programs sometimes are assigned a smaller teaching load. College meteorology/atmospheric science professors publish their research findings in various scholarly journals, such as the *Journal of Applied Meteorology and Climatology*, the *Journal of the Atmospheric Sciences*, the *Journal of Hydrometeorology*, and the *Journal of Climate*. They also write books based on their research or on their own knowledge and experience in the field. Most textbooks are written by college and university teachers. Publishing a significant amount of work has been the traditional standard by which assistant meteorology/atmospheric science professors prove themselves worthy of becoming permanent, tenured faculty.

Typically, pressure to publish is greatest for assistant professors. Pressure to publish increases again if an associate professor wishes to be considered for a promotion to full professorship. Professors in junior colleges face less pressure to publish than those in four-year institutions.

Some faculty members eventually rise to the position of *department chair*, where they govern the affairs of the entire department. Department chairs, faculty, and other professional staff members are aided in their myriad duties by *graduate assistants*, who may help develop teaching materials, conduct research, give examinations, teach lower-level courses, and carry out other activities.

Some college meteorology/atmospheric science professors may also conduct classes in an extension program. In such a program, they teach evening and weekend courses for the benefit of people who otherwise would not be able to take advantage of the institution's resources. They may travel away from the campus and meet with a group of students at another location. They may work full time for the extension division or may divide their time between on-campus and off-campus teaching.

Distance learning programs, an increasingly popular option for students, give meteorology/atmospheric science professors the opportunity to use today's technologies to remain in one place while teaching students who are at a variety of locations simultaneously. The professor's duties, like those when teaching correspondence courses conducted by mail, include grading work that students send in at periodic intervals and advising students of their progress. Computers, the Internet, e-mail, and video conferencing, however, are some of the technology tools that allow professors and students to communicate in "real time" in a virtual classroom setting. Meetings may be scheduled during the same time as traditional classes or during evenings and weekends. Professors who do this work are sometimes known as *extension work, correspondence,* or *distance learning instructors.* They may teach online courses in addition to other classes or may have distance learning as their major teaching responsibility.

The *junior college instructor* has many of the same kinds of responsibilities as does the professor in a four-year college or university. Because junior colleges offer only a two-year program, they teach only undergraduates.

REQUIREMENTS

High School

Your high school's college preparatory program likely includes courses in English, science (especially earth science, physics, biology, and related classes), foreign language, history, math, and government. In addition, you should take courses in speech to get a sense of what it will be like to lecture to a group of students. Your school's

A professor stands on a ladder while constructing a weather monitoring station. *(James Marshall, The Image Works)*

debate team can also help you develop public speaking skills, along with research skills.

Postsecondary Training

At least one advanced degree in meteorology, atmospheric science, or a related field is required to be a professor in a college or university. The master's degree is considered the minimum standard, and graduate work beyond the master's is usually desirable. If you hope to advance in academic rank above instructor, most institutions require a doctorate.

In the last year of your undergraduate program, you'll apply to graduate programs in your area of study. Standards for admission to a graduate program can be high and the competition heavy, depending on the school. Once accepted into a program, your responsibilities will be similar to those of your professors—in addition to attending seminars, you'll research, prepare articles for publication, and teach some undergraduate courses.

You may find employment in a junior college with only a master's degree. Advancement in responsibility and in salary, however, is more likely to come if you have earned a doctorate.

The AMS publishes a listing of schools that offer degree programs in atmospheric and related sciences at its Web site, http://www .ametsoc.org/amsucar_curricula/index.cfm. Another list of education programs can be found at the National Weather Service's Web site, http://www.srh.noaa.gov/jetstream/nws/careers.htm.

Other Requirements

You should enjoy reading, writing, and researching. Not only will you spend many years studying in school, but your whole career will be based on communicating your thoughts and ideas as well. People skills are important because you'll be dealing directly with students, administrators, and other faculty members on a daily basis. You should feel comfortable in a role of authority and possess self-confidence.

EXPLORING

Your high school teachers use many of the same skills as college professors, so talk to your teachers about their careers and their college experiences. You can develop your own teaching experience by volunteering at a community center, working at a day care center, or working at a summer camp (especially one that focuses on meteorology or a related field). Also, spend some time on a college campus to get a sense of the environment. Contact colleges for their admissions brochures and course catalogs (or check them out online); read about the faculty members in meteorology/atmospheric science departments and the courses they teach. Before visiting college campuses, make arrangements to speak to professors who teach courses that interest you. These professors may allow you to sit in on their classes and observe. Also, make appointments with college advisers and with people in the admissions and recruitment offices. If your grades are good enough, you might be able to serve as a teaching assistant during your undergraduate years, which can give you experience leading discussions and grading papers.

EMPLOYERS

Approximately 9,900 postsecondary atmospheric, earth, marine, and space sciences teachers are employed in the United States. Employment opportunities vary based on area of study and education. With a doctorate, a number of publications, and a record of good teaching, professors should find opportunities in universities all across the country. Meteorology/atmospheric science professors teach in undergraduate and graduate programs. The teaching jobs at doctoral institutions are usually better paying and more prestigious. The most sought-after positions are those that offer tenure. Teachers who have only a master's degree will be limited to opportunities with junior colleges, community colleges, and some small private institutions.

STARTING OUT

You should start the process of finding a teaching position while you are in graduate school. The process includes developing a curriculum vitae (a detailed, academic resume), writing for publication, assisting with research, attending conferences, and gaining teaching experience and recommendations. Many students begin applying for teaching positions while finishing their graduate program. For most positions at four-year institutions, you must travel to large conferences where interviews can be arranged with representatives from the universities to which you have applied.

Because of the competition for tenure-track positions, you may have to work for a few years in temporary positions, visiting various schools as an adjunct professor. Some professional associations maintain lists of teaching opportunities in their areas. They may also make lists of applicants available to college administrators looking to fill an available position. Job listings can also be found in the *Chronicle of Higher Education* (http://chronicle.com).

ADVANCEMENT

The normal pattern of advancement is from instructor to assistant professor, to associate professor, to full professor. All four academic ranks are concerned primarily with teaching and research. College faculty members who have an interest in and a talent for administration may be advanced to chair of a department or to dean of their college. A few become college or university presidents or other types of administrators.

The instructor is usually an inexperienced college teacher. He or she may hold a doctorate or may have completed all the Ph.D. requirements except for the dissertation. Most colleges look upon the rank of instructor as the period during which the college is trying out the teacher. Instructors usually are advanced to the position of assistant professors within three to four years. Assistant professors are given up to about six years to prove themselves worthy of tenure, and if they do so, they become associate professors. Some professors choose to remain at the associate level. Others strive to become full professors and receive greater status, salary, and responsibilities.

Most colleges have clearly defined promotion policies from rank to rank for faculty members, and many have written statements about the number of years in which instructors and assistant professors may remain in grade. Administrators in many colleges hope to encourage younger faculty members to increase their skills and competencies and thus to qualify for the more responsible positions of associate professor and full professor.

EARNINGS

Earnings vary by the departments professors work in, by the size of the school, by the type of school (public, private, women's only, for example), and by the level of position the professor holds.

According to the U.S. Department of Labor (DOL), in 2009, the median salary for postsecondary atmospheric, earth, marine, and space sciences teachers was $78,660, with 10 percent earning $133,080 or more and 10 percent earning $43,350 or less. Those employed at junior colleges had mean annual earnings of $73,900. Educators with the highest earnings tend to be senior tenured faculty; those with the lowest earnings are generally graduate assistants. Professors working on the West Coast and the East Coast and those working at doctorate-granting institutions also tend to have the highest salaries. Many professors try to increase their earnings by completing research, publishing in their field, or teaching additional courses.

Benefits for full-time faculty typically include health insurance and retirement funds and, in some cases, stipends for travel related to research, housing allowances, and tuition waivers for dependents.

WORK ENVIRONMENT

A college or university is usually a pleasant place in which to work. Campuses bustle with all types of activities and events, stimulating ideas, and a young, energetic population. Much prestige comes with success as a professor and scholar; professors have the respect of students, colleagues, and others in their community.

Depending on the size of the department, college meteorology/atmospheric science professors may have their own office, or they may have to share an office with one or more colleagues. Their department may provide them with a computer, Internet access, and research assistants. College professors are also able to do much of their office work at home. They can arrange their schedule around class hours, academic meetings, and the established office hours when they meet with students. Most college teachers work more than 40 hours each week. Although college professors may teach only two or three classes a semester, they spend many hours preparing for lectures, examining student work, and conducting research.

OUTLOOK

The DOL predicts that employment for college and university professors will grow faster than the average for all careers through 2018. College enrollment is projected to grow due to an increased number of 18- to 24-year-olds, an increased number of adults returning to college, and an increased number of foreign-born students. Retirement of current faculty members will also provide job openings. However, competition for full-time, tenure-track positions at four-year schools will be very strong. More opportunities will be found at community colleges and in high schools. Employment for atmospheric scientists is expected to grow faster than the average for all careers through 2018, which suggests that there will be strong demand for professors to educate the increasing number of students who plan to enter this field.

A number of factors threaten to change the way colleges and universities hire faculty. Some university leaders are developing more business-based methods of running their schools, focusing on profits and budgets. This can affect college professors in a number of ways. One of the biggest effects is in the replacement of tenure-track faculty positions with part-time instructors. These part-time instructors include adjunct faculty, visiting professors, and graduate students. Organizations such as the American Association of University Professors and the American Federation of Teachers are working to prevent the loss of these full-time jobs, as well as to help part-time instructors receive better pay and benefits. Other issues involve the development of long-distance education departments in many schools. Though these correspondence courses have become very popular in recent years, many professionals believe that students in long-distance education programs receive only a second-rate education. A related concern is about the proliferation of computers in the classroom. Some courses consist only of instruction by computer software and the Internet. The effects of these alternative methods on the teaching profession will be offset somewhat by the expected increases in college enrollment in coming years.

FOR MORE INFORMATION

To read about the issues affecting college professors, contact the following organizations:

American Association of University Professors
1133 19th Street, NW, Suite 200
Washington, DC 20036-3655
Tel: 202-737-5900
E-mail: aaup@aaup.org
http://www.aaup.org

American Federation of Teachers
555 New Jersey Avenue, NW
Washington, DC 20001-2029
Tel: 202-879-4400
http://www.aft.org

The association represents the interests of women in higher education. Visit its Web site for information on scholarships for college students and AAUW Outlook.
American Association of University Women (AAUW)
1111 16th Street, NW
Washington, DC 20036-4809
Tel: 800-326-2289
E-mail: connect@aauw.org
http://www.aauw.org

Visit the society's Web site for information on careers, certification, and membership and scholarships for college students; a searchable database of postsecondary training programs in meteorology; and answers to frequently asked questions about meteorology.

American Meteorological Society
45 Beacon Street
Boston, MA 02108-3693
Tel: 617-227-2425
E-mail: amsinfo@ametsoc.org
http://www.ametsoc.org

For information on industrial and applied meteorology, contact
National Council of Industrial Meteorologists
PO Box 721165
Norman, OK 73070-4892
Tel: 405-329-8707
E-mail: info@ncim.org
http://www.ncim.org

This government agency is concerned with describing and predicting changes in the environment, as well as managing marine and coastal resources. Visit its Web site for details on careers, summer programs and paid internships for young people, and financial aid for college-level students.

National Oceanic and Atmospheric Administration
1401 Constitution Avenue, NW, Room 5128
Washington, DC 20230-0001
http://www.noaa.gov

For information on science education, contact
National Science Teachers Association
1840 Wilson Boulevard
Arlington VA 22201-3092
Tel: 703-243-7100
http://www.nsta.org

Visit the association's Web site for a list of schools with degree programs in meteorology or atmospheric science and information on scholarships and membership for college students.

National Weather Association
228 West Millbrook Road
Raleigh, NC 27609-4304
Tel: 919-845-7121
http://www.nwas.org

The NWS is an agency of the National Oceanic and Atmospheric Administration. Visit its Web site for comprehensive information on weather forecasting and weather phenomena.

National Weather Service (NWS)
1325 East West Highway
Silver Spring, MD 20910-3280
http://www.nws.noaa.gov

This United Nations agency focuses on meteorology (weather and climate), operational hydrology, and related geophysical sciences.

World Meteorological Organization
http://www.wmo.int/pages/index_en.html

═══════ INTERVIEW ═══════

Dr. Fred Carr is the Mark and Kandi McCasland Professor of Meteorology and director of the School of Meteorology at the University of Oklahoma—one of the largest meteorology programs in the United States. He discussed his career and the field of meteorology with the editors of Careers in Focus: Meteorology.

Q. Can you please tell us a little about yourself and your research interests?

A. I grew up in Beverly, Massachusetts, and became interested in meteorology because I was an avid skier and strongly desired all winter storms to produce deep snow. Despite this early area of interest, I earned all my meteorology degrees from Florida State University, and specialized in tropical and monsoon meteorology. After a [postdoctoral position] at State University of New York–Albany, I joined the School of Meteorology faculty at the University of Oklahoma in 1979. My interests broadened to include all of synoptic and mesoscale meteorology, and especially numerical weather prediction. My most rewarding research experiences were when I was able to improve the operational weather forecasting models used by the National Centers for Environmental Prediction. I also enjoy studying interesting weather events and trying to explain how and why they evolved the way they did. For the past 14 years, I have also been the director of the School of Meteorology.

Q. What do you like most and least about being a meteorologist and a meteorology professor?

A. What I like most about being a meteorologist is being able to understand (most of the time!) exactly what is happening with respect to the weather around the country, and being able to make successful forecasts for friends and family. The best part of being a professor is being able to teach and mentor students, and to see them succeed after they leave the university. It is also rewarding to know that your research is benefiting the country on a daily basis. Of course, if your forecasts are wrong, that is one of the least favorite parts of being a meteorologist!

Q. Can you tell us about your program?

A. The School of Meteorology at the University of Oklahoma is one of the largest atmospheric science programs in the country, and more than 70 percent of our undergraduates come from out of state. We have excellent and talented students who go on to many successful careers. We are the top research program at the university, which includes several research centers, a joint university-National Oceanic and Atmospheric Administration (NOAA) institute, and the Oklahoma Climatological Survey. We are all housed together in the National Weather Center (http://nwc.ou.edu) that also contains five NOAA groups, including the National Severe Storms Laboratory, the Storm Prediction Center, and a National Weather Service Forecast Office. Thus many of our students obtain part-time jobs and internships at these organizations while at the University of Oklahoma. In addition to offering the usual B.S., M.S., and Ph.D. degrees, we have a unique M.S. in professional meteorology degree designed to prepare students for private sector meteorology.

Q. What is one thing that young people may not know about a career in meteorology?

A. Many new students in our program hope to become storm-chasers after they graduate. We have to tell them that there are no full-time jobs in storm-chasing, although researchers do this in the spring to make observations that are later studied back in the office. And one can also go storm-chasing as a hobby. The other main thing they learn here is that the field is much broader than they realize, and that many nonweather organizations and companies (such as airlines, insurance, electric power producers, retail outlets, investment firms, etc.) need reliable weather and climate information.

Q. What are the most important personal and professional qualities for meteorologists?

A. In order to earn a meteorology degree, one needs to do well in math and science classes. Thus one should take as much math and physics in high school as possible. Computer skills are also useful, as is some knowledge of geography. In the profession, communication skills, both writing and speaking, are important, as meteorologists often interact with the public or customers. To be a successful researcher, one must have a strong sense of curiosity and desire to do the difficult work of working with millions of meteorological observations to figure out how the atmosphere works.

Q. What is the employment outlook for meteorologists? Have certain areas of the field been especially promising in recent years?

A. The biggest increase in employment in recent years has come from the private sector, as many businesses realize that knowledge of weather and climate in their areas of interest can help them save money. They either make use of one of the 200+ commercial weather companies to provide the weather information they need, or hire meteorologists directly. Television meteorologists are slowly increasing in number although the salaries are not as high since the main networks don't have as many viewers. Employment at the National Weather Service has leveled off since the large increase in the 1990s, but they still need to replace retiring forecasters. The military also employs meteorologists (and provides ROTC scholarships to college students), but not as many as in the past. The demand for research meteorologists and professors (for which you need M.S. and Ph.D. degrees) is pretty strong, especially in the climate area.

Consulting Meteorologists

QUICK FACTS

School Subjects
Earth science
Geography
Physics

Personal Skills
Helping/teaching
Technical/scientific

Work Environment
Primarily indoors
One location with some
travel

Minimum Education Level
Bachelor's degree

Salary Range
$19,650 to $84,710 to $1
million+

Certification or Licensing
Recommended

Outlook
Faster than the average

DOT
025

GOE
02.01.01

NOC
2114

O*NET-SOC
19-2021.00

OVERVIEW

Consulting meteorologists provide weather forecasting and other weather-related services to government agencies and a variety of companies, including sports and recreational businesses, newspapers and television stations, law firms, insurance companies, and Internet weather providers.

HISTORY

Private weather forecasting services became prominent soon after World War II due to the need by private businesses for up-to-date weather forecasts. While the National Weather Service provided weather information, it was not capable of providing the large amount of specialized information required by private companies. Consulting meteorologists provide these services using the latest tools and industry technology.

THE JOB

Consulting meteorologists have many of the same duties as other meteorology professionals. For example, they forecast the weather, predict future climate trends based on past weather systems, and provide expert witness testimony for many legal or insurance cases. However, consulting meteorologists are usually not on staff at a television station, insurance company, or other organization; they provide their services on a contractual basis, or for a per-project fee.

Learn More About It: Extreme Weather

Bluestein, Howard B. *Tornado Alley: Monster Storms of the Great Plains*. New York: Oxford University Press, USA, 2006.

Bologna, Julie, and Christopher K. Passante. *The Complete Idiot's Guide to Extreme Weather*. New York: Alpha, 2006.

Burt, Christopher C. *Extreme Weather: A Guide and Record Book*. Rev. ed. New York: W. W. Norton & Company, 2007.

Emanuel, Kerry A. *Divine Wind: The History and Science of Hurricanes*. New York: Oxford University Press, USA, 2005.

Longshore, David. *Encyclopedia of Hurricanes, Typhoons, and Cyclones*. New York: Checkmark Books, 2008.

Mogil, H. Michael. *Extreme Weather: Understanding the Science of Hurricanes, Tornadoes, Floods, Heat Waves, Snow Storms, Global Warming and Other Atmospheric Disturbances*. New York: Black Dog & Leventhal Publishers, 2007.

The services offered by consulting meteorologists vary depending on the needs of the client. The legal profession makes up the largest client demand for consulting meteorologists. Their professional expertise is often used for civil cases involving severe weather conditions, for example, fatal car crashes during icy conditions or dense fog. Insurance companies rely on a consulting meteorologist's expertise when deciding on weather-related claims, such as claims made as a result of flooding or hail damage. Many times a million-dollar verdict is decided due to the educated opinion of the consulting meteorologist.

Consulting meteorologists also provide daily local forecasts for small television stations or cable channels that do not have a meteorologist on staff. Their forecasts are similar to those given by a full-time broadcast meteorologist, and include maps, charts, radar or satellite images, as well as weather graphics. Radio stations or small regional newspapers may also hire consulting meteorologists to provide daily weather forecasts or to supply information for their print or online weather pages.

Internet weather providers seek the services of consulting meteorologists to provide users with detailed weather forecasts for their particular location. One company, Telemet, offers weather services to customers in the United States, South America, and parts of Europe. Telemet meteorologists can deliver customized weather data in various languages and computer formats. Depending on how in-depth the information needed, customers can choose hourly text forecasts, weather displays that include 3D graphics, satellite images, as well as data and stream videos.

Construction companies, large landscape businesses, and utility companies often hire consulting meteorologists to help them schedule work sessions. By having daily forecasts pinpointing the weather according to the work site's location, company managers can add staff during good weather, and choose to trim daily staff or cancel scheduled work during inclement weather. Winery owners also hire consulting meteorologists to help them determine the best time to plant and harvest their grapes.

Recreational companies also rely on the weather advice of consultants. In addition to the daily weather for their locality, ski resort managers can also request information such as the amount and type of snow expected in their area. Golf courses can post information received, including wind direction and velocity or risk of approaching thunderstorms. Beach resorts can request weather information such as water temperature, estimated sunburn times, and daily ozone levels.

Environmental groups hire consulting meteorologists to help conduct research on various weather-related issues, such as air pollution.

Consulting meteorologists, especially those who are freelancers, often have other duties aside from weather forecasting. They conduct their own research and experiments, and in some cases, create charts, maps, and graphics that detail their findings. They may be responsible for marketing their services to prospective clients, as well as handling clerical duties such as office paper work or billing for completed projects.

REQUIREMENTS

High School
Take as many mathematics, science (especially physics, earth science, and chemistry), geography, and computer science classes as possible to prepare for college study. You will also need strong communication skills, so be sure to take English and speech classes. As a consulting meteorologist, you will frequently write reports, discuss forecasts and research with colleagues and clients, and even possibly testify in court or provide forecasts on radio or television newscasts.

Postsecondary Training
Individuals offering consulting services have a minimum of a bachelor's degree in meteorology, another atmospheric science, earth science, or a related field. Meteorologists in managerial and other

upper-level positions often have graduate degrees. Students often complete one or more internship as part of their education. Internships allow students to explore career options and make valuable

An agricultural meteorologist (*right*) and another scientist analyze a remote-sensing map of a field study of corn and soybean crop yields in Illinois. *(Scott Bauer, Agricultural Research Service, USDA)*

contacts that could lead to future job opportunities. Visit http://
www.ametsoc.org/amsstudentinfo/internships.html for a list of
internship opportunities.

The American Meteorological Society (AMS) publishes a list of
schools that offer degree programs in atmospheric and related sciences at its Web site, http://www.ametsoc.org/amsucar_curricula/
index.cfm. Another list of education programs can be found at the
National Weather Service's Web site, http://www.srh.noaa.gov/
jetstream/nws/careers.htm.

For entry-level positions in the federal government, you must have
a bachelor's degree (not necessarily in meteorology) with at least 24
semester hours of meteorology courses, including six hours in the
analysis and prediction of weather systems and two hours of remote
sensing of the atmosphere or instrumentation. Other required courses
include calculus, physics, and other physical science courses, such as
statistics, computer science, chemistry, physical oceanography, and
physical climatology. Advanced graduate training in meteorology
and related areas is required for research and teaching positions, as
well as for other high-level positions in meteorology. Many managers and top researchers have doctorates.

Because the armed forces require the services of so many meteorologists, they have programs to send recently commissioned, new
college graduates to civilian universities for intensive training in
meteorology.

Certification or Licensing

The AMS confers the certified consulting meteorologist designation
to meteorologists who meet educational requirements, have at least
five years' experience in the field, meet character requirements, and
pass an examination. Contact the society for more information.

The AMS and the National Weather Association (NWA) each offer
certification to broadcast meteorologists. To qualify for the AMS Seal
of Approval, you must meet educational requirements and demonstrate scientific competence and effective communication skills. You
must submit recorded samples of your work for review by an evaluation board. Requirements for the NWA Seal of Approval are similar,
but you must also have a certain amount of on-air experience and
pass a written exam. Although the AMS and the NWA seals are not
required for broadcast meteorologists to work in this field, you will
have an advantage when looking for a job if you hold these seals. Some
TV and radio stations note that their forecaster has a seal of approval
in their advertisements.

Other Requirements

Successful consulting meteorologists are organized, have excellent research skills, and are able to work well under pressure in order to meet deadlines. They are able to communicate complex theories and events, orally and in writing. They must be able to absorb pertinent information quickly and pass it on to coworkers and their employers. Meteorologists who work in broadcasting must have especially good communication and time-management skills in order to deal with the pressure and deadlines of the newsroom. If they appear on television, they should be well groomed and have no nervous mannerisms. Consulting meteorologists who are self-employed must have excellent business skills and the drive and ambition to build their businesses.

EXPLORING

There are several ways that you can explore career paths in meteorology. Each year, for example, the federal government's National Weather Service accepts a limited number of student volunteers, mostly college students but also a few high school students. Some universities offer credit for a college student's volunteer work in connection with meteorology courses. The National Oceanic and Atmospheric Administration has details about the volunteer program and other methods of career exploration at its Web site, http://www.volunteer.noaa.gov.

Arrange for an information interview with a meteorologist or a meteorology professor. Your high school counselor should be able to help you set up this meeting. You can also get additional information from organizations, such as those listed at the end of this article.

The American Meteorological Society offers a comprehensive career guide on its Web site, http://www.ametsoc.org/atmoscareers. Content includes suggestions on the types of course work and training to consider during the college years, various career opportunities, typical employers and workplaces, job and salary outlook statistics, and certification information.

You can also read books about meteorology. Here are a few suggestions: *The American Meteorological Society Weather Book: The Ultimate Guide to America's Weather,* by Jack Williams (Chicago: University of Chicago Press, 2009); *Meteorology Today: An Introduction to Weather, Climate, and the Environment,* 9th edition, by C. Donald Ahrens (Florence, Ky.: Brooks Cole, 2008); and *Weather Whys: Facts, Myths, and Oddities,* by Paul Yeager (New York: Perigee Trade, 2010). Ask your school or community librarian to provide more suggestions.

EMPLOYERS

Consulting meteorologists work for private weather consulting firms, engineering service firms, law firms, insurance companies, construction companies, large landscape businesses, utility companies, shipping companies, Internet weather providers, newspapers, recreational companies, commercial airlines, radio and television stations, and any other organization that needs weather forecasts or meteorological information.

STARTING OUT

You won't start out in your career as a consulting meteorologist. It usually takes a couple of years working as a general meteorologist to gain experience before you can advertise your expertise as a consulting meteorologist.

You can find job leads through your college's career services office and through contacts you have made with professors and during internships. Additionally, the American Meteorological Society (http://www.ametsoc.org/careercenter) and National Weather Association (http://www.nwas.org/jobs.php) provide job listings at their Web sites.

ADVANCEMENT

Most consulting meteorologists are self-employed. As such, they do not follow a traditional advancement path. They advance by building their businesses and attracting more clients—which often results in higher earnings and the chance to work on more prestigious assignments. Consulting meteorologists who are employed by government agencies advance according to civil service regulations. Those in the private sector can earn higher salaries and promotions, or they may be asked to work on more demanding projects.

EARNINGS

The U.S. Department of Labor (DOL) reports that median annual earnings of atmospheric scientists were $84,710 in 2009. Salaries ranged from less than $40,560 to more than $127,250. The average salary for meteorologists employed by the federal government was $94,210. Those who worked for scientific research and development services earned $87,180 annually.

Meteorologists with a bachelor of science degree are usually hired by the National Weather Service at the GS-5 to GS-7 grade levels;

base salaries at these levels ranged from $27,431 (GS-5), to $30,577 (GS-6), to $33,979 (GS-7) in 2010. Those with a master of science degree enter at the GS-7 to GS-9 levels, which had base pay that ranged from $33,979 (GS-7), to $37,631 (GS-8), to $41,563 (GS-9). Meteorologists with Ph.D.'s enter at the GS-9 to GS-11 levels, which ranged from $41,563 (GS-9), to $45,771 (GS-10), to $50,287 (GS-11).

Broadcast meteorologists earned mean annual salaries of $85,760 in 2009, according to the DOL. Salaries ranged from less than $19,650 to more than $1 million a year.

Benefits for meteorologists depend on the employer; however, they usually include such items as health insurance, retirement or 401(k) plans, and paid vacation days.

WORK ENVIRONMENT

Weather forecasts and related information are needed 24 hours a day, seven days a week. This means that some consulting meteorologists, often on a rotating basis, work evenings and weekends. Others have traditional 9-to-5 schedules.

Work settings vary for consulting meteorologists. Some work in traditional offices or at weather stations. Others work at broadcast stations or travel to courthouses to testify about their findings. Some travel to remote locations to collect research is required for certain positions. Field research may require consulting meteorologists to spend considerable time away from home and work in occasionally primitive conditions.

OUTLOOK

According to the *Occupational Outlook Handbook*, employment for meteorologists should grow faster than the average for all careers through 2018. Despite this prediction, there will be strong competition for jobs. Consulting meteorologists who are certified and have experience in a variety of meteorological specialties will have the best employment prospects.

FOR MORE INFORMATION

For information on forensic careers and education, contact
American Academy of Forensic Sciences
410 North 21st Street
Colorado Springs, CO 80904-2712
Tel: 719-636-1100
http://www.aafs.org

Visit the society's Web site for information on careers, certification, and membership and scholarships for college students; a searchable database of postsecondary training programs in meteorology; and answers to frequently asked questions about meteorology.

American Meteorological Society
45 Beacon Street
Boston, MA 02108-3693
Tel: 617-227-2425
E-mail: amsinfo@ametsoc.org
http://www.ametsoc.org

The association provides information on broadcast education, scholarships for college students, jobs, and useful publications at its Web site.

National Association of Broadcasters
1771 N Street, NW
Washington, DC 20036-2800
Tel: 202-429-5300
E-mail: nab@nab.org
http://www.nab.org

For information on industrial and applied meteorology, contact
National Council of Industrial Meteorologists
PO Box 721165
Norman, OK 73070-4892
Tel: 405-329-8707
E-mail: info@ncim.org
http://www.ncim.org

The National Oceanic and Atmospheric Administration says that its reach "goes from the surface of the sun to the depths of the ocean floor." Visit its Web site for information on careers, summer programs and paid internships for young people, and financial aid for college-level students.

National Oceanic and Atmospheric Administration
1401 Constitution Avenue, NW, Room 5128
Washington, DC 20230-0001
http://www.noaa.gov

Visit the association's Web site for a list of schools with degree programs in meteorology or atmospheric science and information on scholarships and membership for college students.

National Weather Association
228 West Millbrook Road
Raleigh, NC 27609-4304
Tel: 919-845-7121
http://www.nwas.org

*The NWS is an agency of the National Oceanic and Atmospheric
Administration. Visit its Web site for comprehensive information
on weather forecasting and weather phenomena.*
National Weather Service (NWS)
1325 East West Highway
Silver Spring, MD 20910-3280
http://www.nws.noaa.gov

*This United Nations agency focuses on meteorology (weather and
climate), operational hydrology, and related geophysical sciences.*
World Meteorological Organization
http://www.wmo.int/pages/index_en.html

Environmental Meteorologists

OVERVIEW

Environmental meteorologists study the physical characteristics, movements, and processes of weather. They are also concerned with how environmental problems affect our weather. Their research is used by many industries, including agriculture, forestry, transportation, and defense. Government and private environmental groups also rely on their research to study climate trends such as global warming and ozone depletion.

HISTORY

While people have studied the atmosphere since the days of the ancient Greek philosopher Aristotle, concerns about environmental changes and our human contribution to these shifts is a more recent line of study.

The most notable legislation in this arena is the Clean Air Act, originally drafted in 1970 to address air pollution and most recently amended in 1990 to better protect and improve air quality. The current law focuses on the following: reducing emissions of toxic air pollutants that are known to, or are suspected of, causing cancer or other serious health problems; reducing outdoor air pollutants that cause smog, haze, acid rain, and environmental hazards; and phasing out production and use of chemicals that destroy the earth's ozone layer. Environmental meteorologists were consulted to draft this powerful legislation. Their research points out that we are to blame for much of the pollutants in our atmosphere, from the emissions from our cars that we drive, to those discharged by our manufacturing plants and factories.

Another more recent line of thinking is that protecting our environment is not just a national priority, but also a global one. International cooperation is key to making the greatest impact. For this purpose, specialized weather centers are stationed around the world that pass Doppler radar and satellite information through what is called the Global Telecommunications System, which was created by the World Meteorological Organization. These centers observe local conditions and develop large computer-model simulations.

Environmental meteorology research programs have also gone international. For example, the Global Energy and Water Cycle Experiment is an international effort to understand climate variability through the study of energy and water cycles running through our atmosphere, land, and oceans. The Tropical Rainfall Measuring Mission, a joint effort by NASA and Japan Aerospace Exploration

Learn More About It

Aguado, Edward, and James E. Burt. *Understanding Weather and Climate.* 5th ed. Upper Saddle River, N.J.: Prentice Hall, 2009.

Ahrens, C. Donald. *Meteorology Today: An Introduction to Weather, Climate, and the Environment.* 9th ed. Florence, Ky.: Brooks Cole, 2008.

Brinkley, Douglas. *The Great Deluge: Hurricane Katrina, New Orleans, and the Mississippi Gulf Coast.* New York: Harper Perennial, 2007.

Dunlop, Storm. *The Weather Identification Handbook: The Ultimate Guide for Weather Watchers.* Guilford, Conn.: The Lyons Press, 2003.

Emanuel, Kerry A. *Divine Wind: The History and Science of Hurricanes.* New York: Oxford University Press, USA, 2005.

Hile, Kevin. *The Handy Weather Answer Book.* 2d ed. Canton, Mich.: Visible Ink Press, 2009.

Lutgens, Frederick K. *The Atmosphere: An Introduction to Meteorology.* 11th ed. Upper Saddle River, N.J.: Prentice Hall, 2009.

Williams, Jack. *The American Meteorological Society Weather Book: The Ultimate Guide to America's Weather.* Chicago: University of Chicago Press, 2009.

Yeager, Paul. *Weather Whys: Facts, Myths, and Oddities.* New York: Perigee Trade, 2010.

Agency, is designed to monitor and study tropical rainfall from space.

THE JOB

We cannot survive without water and air, so it's important to have these resources available and in the best condition possible for current and future generations. Environmental meteorologists study and help protect these resources. Not only do they study the characteristics, processes, and patterns of various types of weather, but also how these forces affect the rest of our environment and our quality of life.

For example, environmental meteorologists are concerned with how weather can affect agriculture or any other weather-sensitive industry. They may study decades' worth of temperature averages, rainfall, and levels of solar radiation using meteorological databases or weather archives. Using this information, as well as other meteorological tools, such as satellite and radar imagery, maps and charts, and ground samples, they can identify climate variability according to specific locations. Climate variability is any social or economic correlations to variation in weather and climate. Farmers and other agricultural specialists rely on the work done by environmental meteorologists to estimate crop yields, manage crops, and otherwise ensure that harvests will be bountiful. In South Carolina, for example, environmental meteorologists have helped peanut farmers prepare for the upcoming growing season by using model forecast data that targets the threat of peanut mold. In fact, environmental meteorologists have introduced AgroClimate, an interactive Web site that uses climate information to help improve agricultural output.

Environmental meteorologists are also concerned with the impact of human-made pollution on the weather and atmosphere, and conduct research on topics such as environmental and atmospheric pollution, the shortage of fresh water in certain areas, and air quality. For example, meteorologists may conduct research on a country's energy usage and its affect on air and water pollution. How much does a country's dependence on fossil fuels, resulting in carbon emissions, have an impact on the food production and water availability in that nation? Meteorologists may also conduct studies on how this pollution behaves once it is released into the atmosphere. Does pollution behave differently depending on its type as well as the humidity, heat, and wind and precipitation patterns of the season and/or geographic location? Thanks to the research findings of environmental meteorologists, communities are able to better monitor—and improve—existing pollution control systems.

Some environmental meteorologists may be employed by environmental groups and various industries to test the emissions released by automobiles, coal plants, and factories. Their data, compiled into an environmental impact report, is often used to force offending companies to change their business practices. Other areas of study for environmental meteorologists may include global warming trends and ozone zone depletion. For example, by conducting tests and monitoring ozone levels, they can advise government agencies regarding instances of "unhealthy thresholds" that occur when air pollution, combined with summer heat, causes air quality to go below environmental standards. When these thresholds are breached, government agencies issue health alerts regarding poor air quality.

The work of environmental meteorologists is often used as important reference by the construction and engineering industries. Their research on the climate and air quality of urban areas can be used by developers when conducting project planning. Some of the research

An environmental meteorologist collects data on a tower that has been built over the Amazon rainforest in Brazil. *(Luiz C. Marigo, Peter Arnold Images/Photolibrary)*

and services offered by environmental meteorologists include evaluation of air quality and human-biometeorology, including ventilation paths and urban green spaces, and creating synthetic climatic function maps or planning advice maps.

In addition, many environmental meteorologists have other duties, including maintaining research databases, compiling statistics and research into written or electronic reports, and creating graphs, charts, or weather maps. Some environmental meteorologists meet with government or industry officials to present their findings and give recommendations. Others work as teachers at colleges and universities. Still others write books and articles about the field.

REQUIREMENTS

High School

You can best prepare for a college major in meteorology by taking high school courses in mathematics, geography, biology, environmental and earth science, computer science, physics, and chemistry. English and speech classes are also very important since environmental meteorologists need strong communication skills.

Postsecondary Training

Although some beginners in meteorological work have majored in subjects related to meteorology, the usual minimal requirement for work in this field is a bachelor's degree in meteorology. For entry-level positions in the federal government, you must have a bachelor's degree (not necessarily in meteorology) with at least 24 semester hours of meteorology courses, including six hours in the analysis and prediction of weather systems and two hours of remote sensing of the atmosphere or instrumentation. Other required courses include calculus, physics, and other physical science courses, such as statistics, computer science, chemistry, physical oceanography, and physical climatology. Advanced graduate training in meteorology and related areas is required for research and teaching positions, as well as for other high-level positions in meteorology. High-level personnel typically have doctorates.

Many meteorology students participate in internships to gain hands-on experience in the field before graduation. Visit http://www.ametsoc.org/amsstudentinfo/internships.html for a list of internship opportunities.

The American Meteorological Society (AMS) publishes a list of schools that offer degree programs in atmospheric and related sciences

at its Web site, http://www.ametsoc.org/amsucar_curricula/index
.cfm. Another list of education programs can be found at the National
Weather Service's Web site, http://www.srh.noaa.gov/jetstream/nws/
careers.htm.

Certification or Licensing
The AMS confers the certified consulting meteorologist designation
to meteorologists who meet educational requirements, have at least
five years' experience in the field, meet character requirements, and
pass an examination. Contact the society for more information.

Other Requirements
To be a successful environmental meteorologist, you should enjoy
conducting research, be able to communicate effectively orally and
in writing, have good organizational skills, enjoy solving problems,
and have a passion for protecting the environment.

EXPLORING

Your first step in learning about meteorology is just outside your
front door, where you can observe a variety of meteorological phenomena. Study and record weather in your area.

Ask your science teacher or a counselor to arrange an information interview with an environmental meteorologist. Visit the Web
sites of college meteorology programs to read about typical classes,
internships, and degree requirements. Participate in school science
clubs and competitions.

The AMS offers a comprehensive career guide on its Web site,
http://www.ametsoc.org/atmoscareers. Content includes suggestions on the types of course work and training to consider during
the college years, various career opportunities, typical employers
and workplaces, job and salary outlook statistics, and certification
information.

EMPLOYERS

The federal government is the largest employer of environmental
meteorologists. State government agencies and climate offices also
hire meteorologists. Others work for private environmental organizations, colleges and universities, and any industry that requires
environmental-related meteorological research.

Weather Cooling

Can the method in which farmers arrange their crops combat global warming? That is the question climate scientists in the Midwest are pondering as they notice a curious cooling trend taking place in the historically dog days of summer.

According to the *Chicago Tribune*, between 1930 and 1939, the city of Chicago recorded 344 days of 90+ degree weather during the months of July and August. Between 2000 and 2009, that number dropped to just 172 days during the same months.

One big change that has occurred in that time is more efficient planting methods. Farmers today are able to yield more crops in less space. The average width between rows of corn shrunk from 40 inches to 30 inches in the last 50 years. Some farmers can produce more than 200 bushels of corn from one acre of land, more than twice what an average farmer produced in the 1970s.

How does this affect the weather? Research shows that more densely packed crops release more water vapor into the atmosphere, raising the dew point, and cooling the average temperature in the area. Further research is needed but now scientists are hoping to discover whether intentional intense farming, such as densely packed rows of sugar cane, could be used to reverse warming trends seen in South America or other areas of the world. This planting technique is an exciting discovery as scientists search for solutions to global warming.

STARTING OUT

Many environmental meteorologists land their first jobs in the field as a result of contacts made during internships or fellowships. College professors and career services offices may also be able to provide job leads. Employment opportunities can also be found via direct application to government agencies and private companies that employ environmental meteorologists. Additionally, the American Meteorological Society (http://www.ametsoc.org/careercenter) and National Weather Association (http://www.nwas.org/jobs.php) provide job listings at their Web sites.

ADVANCEMENT

Environmental meteorologists typically advance by receiving higher pay, managerial responsibilities, or professional recognition for their work. Some meteorologists go into business for themselves by establishing their own consulting services. Meteorologists who are employed in teaching and research in colleges and universities advance through academic promotions or by taking on administrative titles, such as department head or dean of students.

EARNINGS

Atmospheric scientists earned median annual salaries of $84,710 in 2009, according to the U.S. Department of Labor. Salaries ranged from less than $40,560 to more than $127,250. The average salary for meteorologists employed by the federal government was $94,210.

Meteorologists with a bachelor of science degree are usually hired by the National Weather Service at the GS-5 to GS-7 grade levels; base salaries at these levels ranged from $27,431 (GS-5), to $30,577 (GS-6), to $33,979 (GS-7) in 2010. Those with a master of science degree enter at the GS-7 to GS-9 levels, which had base pay that ranged from $33,979 (GS-7), to $37,631 (GS-8), to $41,563 (GS-9). Meteorologists with Ph.D.'s enter at the GS-9 to GS-11 levels, which ranged from $41,563 (GS-9), to $45,771 (GS-10), to $50,287 (GS-11).

Depending on their employers, most environmental meteorologists enjoy a full complement of benefits, including vacation and sick time as well as holidays and medical and dental insurance. Self-employed workers must provide their own benefits.

WORK ENVIRONMENT

Work environments range from clean, comfortable offices to primitive research camps, where the amenities of home are unavailable. When conducting field research, environmental meteorologists may be away from home for long periods of time and work in close quarters with other scientists. Environmental meteorologists who work as college professors enjoy the benefits of the nine-month academic calendar and have time in the summer to conduct research or pursue other interests.

OUTLOOK

There are many major environmental problems in the world, which suggests that there will continue to be strong demand for environmental meteorologists. According to the *Occupational Outlook Handbook*, overall employment for meteorologists should grow faster than the average for all careers through 2018. Despite this prediction, there will be strong competition for jobs. Overall, environmental meteorologists with advanced degrees and certification will have the best chances of landing a good job.

FOR MORE INFORMATION

Visit the society's Web site for information on careers, certification, and membership and scholarships for college students; a searchable database of postsecondary training programs in meteorology; and answers to frequently asked questions about meteorology.

American Meteorological Society
45 Beacon Street
Boston, MA 02108-3693
Tel: 617-227-2425
E-mail: amsinfo@ametsoc.org
http://www.ametsoc.org

The society offers information on careers, volunteer positions, publications, and internships and jobs for college students. It also offers diversity programs to encourage students of color to enter the field.

American Society of Limnology and Oceanography
5400 Bosque Boulevard, Suite 680
Waco, TX 76710-4446
Tel: 800-929-2756
E-mail: business@aslo.org
http://www.aslo.org

The National Oceanic and Atmospheric Administration says that its reach "goes from the surface of the sun to the depths of the ocean floor." Visit its Web site for information on environmental topics such as climate monitoring, global warming, fisheries management, and coastal restoration, as well as details on careers, summer programs and paid internships for young people, and financial aid for college-level students.

National Oceanic and Atmospheric Administration
1401 Constitution Avenue, NW, Room 5128
Washington, DC 20230-0001
http://www.noaa.gov

Visit the association's Web site for a list of schools with degree programs in meteorology or atmospheric science and information on scholarships and membership for college students.

National Weather Association
228 West Millbrook Road
Raleigh, NC 27609-4304
Tel: 919-845-7121
http://www.nwas.org

The NWS is an agency of the National Oceanic and Atmospheric Administration. Visit its Web site for comprehensive information on weather forecasting and weather phenomena.
National Weather Service (NWS)
1325 East West Highway
Silver Spring, MD 20910-3280
http://www.nws.noaa.gov

This United Nations agency focuses on meteorology (weather and climate), operational hydrology, and related geophysical sciences.
World Meteorological Organization
http://www.wmo.int/pages/index_en.html

Forensic Meteorologists

QUICK FACTS

School Subjects
Earth science
Geography
Physics

Personal Skills
Technical/scientific

Work Environment
Indoors and outdoors
Primarily multiple locations

Minimum Education Level
Bachelor's degree

Salary Range
$40,560 to $84,710 to
$127,250+

Certification or Licensing
Recommended

Outlook
About as fast as the average

DOT
025

GOE
02.01.01

NOC
2114

O*NET-SOC
19-2021.00

OVERVIEW

The American Academy of Forensic Sciences defines forensic science as any science that is "used in public, in a court, or in the justice system." *Forensic meteorologists* are specially trained meteorologists who use their expertise to investigate, report, re-create, and provide testimony regarding past weather conditions. Their services are used by law firms, insurance companies, and government agencies to help settle lawsuits, criminal investigations, insurance claims, and environmental regulatory actions.

HISTORY

While forensic meteorology as a career specialty may have only surfaced in the last 30 years or so, the practice of applying weather and related knowledge to legal matters is not a new concept. As early as 1900, according to *Weatherwise*, Professor H. J. Cox, head of the U.S. Weather Bureau's Chicago office, reported the following: "Since the opening of the present term of court, last fall, I have been in court 33 times to testify as to the condition of the weather at a particular time and as to what bearing it might have on the case at issue. In addition to these 33 cases, many cases are settled out of court on the records of the weather department. Such cases are principally damage suits arising from the shipment of perishable goods. Every day we have from eight to 10 telephone calls and numerous letters from commission merchants asking as to the weather conditions on particular dates, and the claims are usually settled accordingly."

Following the emergence of other meteorology careers, the specialty field of forensic meteorology grew steadily after World War II.

Financial Aid for Aspiring Meteorologists

The American Meteorological Society offers several scholarships to high school seniors and college students. The AMS/Industry Minority Scholarship is open to minority students who have been traditionally underrepresented in the sciences, especially Native American, Hispanic, and Black/African-American students. Applicants must be high school seniors who plan to pursue a career in the atmospheric or related oceanic and hydrologic sciences. The AMS/Freshman Undergraduate Scholarship is available to high school seniors who plan to study atmospheric or related oceanic or hydrologic sciences in college. Visit http://www.ametsoc.org/amsstudentinfo/scholfeldocs for more information and to download applications.

To encourage growth in the field, the American Meteorological Society (AMS) sponsored the first conference on forensic meteorology in 1976. Presentations and panel discussions were led by members of both the meteorological and legal professions.

Still today, while many meteorologists offer forensic services along with other specialties such as forecasting or applied research, very few specialize solely in forensics. However, the growth and popularity of the Internet has made forensic meteorology extremely accessible. Currently, online weather services provide online claim forms for forensic meteorological services to lawyers, insurance claim adjusters, government agencies, and more.

THE JOB

A town braces itself for a severe windstorm forecast to hit in a matter of hours. Yet despite all precautions, a portion of a shopping mall's outdoor sign breaks off, seriously injuring the occupants of a passing vehicle. Are the shopping mall owners to blame for this accident? Or was the unfortunate event simply an "act of God," with all injury claims covered by the mall's insurance provider? The answer lies with the research and reporting done by forensic meteorologists.

Forensic meteorologists use their expertise in collecting standard weather observations and processing weather data through radar and satellite imagery to create a report about the weather conditions at a particular location, day, or time. Their services are highly sought after by law firms, insurance companies, and government agencies to help settle civil lawsuits and insurance claims, solve transportation accidents, and address environmental regulatory actions. They may also be called to testify or provide evidence during trials that involve murder, charges of negligence, or other alleged crimes.

Many forensic meteorologists provide expert analysis for insurance claims. Their opinion counts heavily when determining whether pending claims were the result of negligence or Mother Nature. Forensic meteorologists working on the shopping mall sign incident, for example, could check the hourly data taken at the National Weather Service station closest to the mall's location on the day of the storm. Any changes in temperature, wind speed, and wind direction would signal a strong cold front entering the area. They could also check monthly data recorded for the area relating to climatological conditions. If there were no storms ever recorded of the same magnitude and wind intensity, forensic meteorologists could testify that the storm in question was rare, and thus could qualify as "an act of God." In this case, the mall owners were not found negligent, and all injury claims were covered by their insurance policy.

Forensic meteorologists may also be hired by insurance companies to work on other types of cases such as automobile accidents or property damage, or by law firms for personal injury or civil cases. They may need to investigate or re-create weather patterns specific to the location or time in question using airport weather reports, Doppler radar records, or satellite images. Their research can indicate the amount of snow or ice on ground surfaces at a given time; identify temperature extremes, heavy precipitation and flooding problems; and help gauge the severity of windstorms, tornados, and hurricanes. When working on a case involving hail damage, they may refer to information gathered by HailTrax, a product that provides radar mapping for hail falls. For lightning damage, forensic meteorologists may obtain information from the National Lightning Detection Network, which pinpoints the exact location and time of lightning strikes. However, since weather reports often cover large areas, forensic meteorologists may need to re-create a microclimate report. They may use information from local weather monitoring resources, or even eyewitnesses, to re-create the weather conditions of a small area at a particular time. For example, eyewitnesses may give testimony to dense fog or unusually blinding sunlight at the time of an automobile accident.

Forensic meteorologists often make site visits to determine if ground conditions could have played a role in the accident or crime. Once the data is gathered, they compile their research into an unbiased, easy-to-understand report that is used by insurance adjusters or by lawyers during depositions, hearings, or other court proceedings. Forensic meteorologists provide expert testimony via telephone or video recording, or they may testify in court during a trial.

Environmental firms also rely on the expertise of forensic meteorologists when conducting air quality research and controls. For example, before a new power plant can be built, environmental agencies will conduct tests to determine the amount of pollutants the structure is expected to release. Working with a team of chemists and other scientists, forensic meteorologists can create a software model to predict the emission and ozone levels caused by the power plant.

Many forensic meteorologists are self-employed, or work for a company that specializes in providing forensic meteorology services. Others are employed directly by law firms, insurance companies, and government agencies.

REQUIREMENTS

High School
In high school, take courses in mathematics, geography, computer science, law, physics, and chemistry. English and speech classes will help you to develop your communication skills, which you will use frequently when interacting with coworkers and witnesses, writing reports, and testifying during legal proceedings.

Postsecondary Training
Forensic meteorologists have at least a bachelor's degree in meteorology, another atmospheric science, earth science, or a related field. Many forensic meteorologists have advanced degrees in meteorology. They learn much of the forensic science-related aspects of their job by participating in seminars, conferences, and on-the-job training with experienced forensic meteorologists.

Certification or Licensing
The American Meteorological Society confers the certified consulting meteorologist designation to meteorologists who meet educational requirements, have at least five years' experience in the field, meet character requirements, and pass an examination. Contact the society for more information on certification requirements.

Other Requirements
To be a successful forensic meteorologist, you should have excellent analytical skills and be very attentive to detail. You should have

strong communication and interpersonal skills in order to inter-act well with witnesses, other meteorologists, attorneys, and law enforcement officers, as well as testify during court proceedings. Other key traits for forensic meteorologists include fairness, honesty, curiosity, and strong organizational skills. Those who are self-employed must have strong business skills.

EXPLORING

To learn more about forensic meteorology, visit the Web sites of meteorology associations. The American Meteorological Society offers a comprehensive career guide on its Web site, http://www.ametsoc.org/atmoscareers. Content includes suggestions on the types of course work and training to consider during the college years, various career opportunities (including those in forensic meteorology), typical employers and workplaces, job and salary outlook statistics, and certification information. You can also participate in an information interview with a forensic meteorologist. Ask your school counselor or science teacher to help arrange the interview, or contact professional associations for potential interview leads. Finally, you can also read books about meteorology such as *The American Meteorological Society Weather Book: The Ultimate Guide to America's Weather*, by Jack Williams (Chicago: University of Chicago Press, 2009). Ask your school or community librarian to provide more suggestions.

EMPLOYERS

Forensic meteorologists are employed by law firms, insurance companies, environmental firms, and government agencies.

STARTING OUT

The career of forensic meteorologist is typically not an entry-level job. It takes years of experience to build a reputation as a qualified forensic meteorologist. Most people who are interested in a career in forensic meteorology first work as traditional meteorologists. They gradually gain experience and contacts before advertising their expertise in forensic meteorology. Job leads for meteorologists can be obtained via college career services offices, the Web sites of professional associations, and advertisements in meteorology periodicals. They can also be obtained from contacts made during internships or by contacting private companies and government agencies that employ meteorologists.

ADVANCEMENT

Forensic meteorologists who work as full-time employees advance by receiving pay raises and managerial responsibilities. Self-employed forensic meteorologists advance by gaining professional recognition for the quality of their work, earning higher incomes, expanding their businesses, and being hired to work on higher-profile cases.

EARNINGS

The U.S. Department of Labor reports that median annual earnings of atmospheric scientists (including forensic meteorologists) were $84,710 in 2009. Salaries ranged from less than $40,560 to more than $127,250. The average salary for meteorologists employed by the federal government was $94,210. Those who worked for scientific research and development services earned $87,180 a year.

Depending on their employers, most forensic meteorologists enjoy a full complement of benefits, including vacation and sick time as well as holidays and medical and dental insurance. Self-employed workers must provide their own benefits.

WORK ENVIRONMENT

Work settings for forensic meteorologists vary by employer and job duties. Some meteorologists spend most of their day in offices analyzing data and preparing reports. Others frequently travel to crime or accident scenes to observe weather conditions and gather information. They also testify in court or provide depositions. Courtrooms can sometimes be tense places, and forensic meteorologists must be able to defend their findings under occasionally harsh questioning from defense attorneys or other individuals involved in the case.

OUTLOOK

Employment for meteorologists should grow faster than the average for all careers through 2018, according to the *Occupational Outlook Handbook*. Job opportunities will not be as strong for forensic meteorologists. Many people want to enter this fascinating field. Most forensic meteorologists only work part time, with the remainder of their time spent employed as traditional meteorologists or in another specialized meteorology field. Forensic meteorologists with experience and advanced education will have the best chances of building a full-time career in this specialty.

FOR MORE INFORMATION

For information on forensic careers and education, contact
American Academy of Forensic Sciences
410 North 21st Street
Colorado Springs, CO 80904-2712
Tel: 719-636-1100
http://www.aafs.org

Visit the society's Web site for information on careers, certification, and membership and scholarships for college students; a searchable database of postsecondary training programs in meteorology; and answers to frequently asked questions about meteorology.
American Meteorological Society
45 Beacon Street
Boston, MA 02108-3693
Tel: 617-227-2425
E-mail: amsinfo@ametsoc.org
http://www.ametsoc.org

For information on industrial and applied meteorology, contact
National Council of Industrial Meteorologists
PO Box 721165
Norman, OK 73070-4892
Tel: 405-329-8707
E-mail: info@ncim.org
http://www.ncim.org

This government agency is concerned with describing and predicting changes in the environment, as well as managing marine and coastal resources. Visit its Web site for details on careers, summer programs and paid internships for young people, and financial aid for college-level students.
National Oceanic and Atmospheric Administration
1401 Constitution Avenue, NW, Room 5128
Washington, DC 20230-0001
http://www.noaa.gov

Visit the association's Web site for a list of schools with degree programs in meteorology or atmospheric science and information on scholarships and membership for college students.

National Weather Association
228 West Millbrook Road
Raleigh, NC 27609-4304
Tel: 919-845-7121
http://www.nwas.org

*The NWS is an agency of the National Oceanic and Atmospheric
Administration. Visit its Web site for information on weather forecasting and weather phenomena.*
National Weather Service (NWS)
1325 East West Highway
Silver Spring, MD 20910-3280
http://www.nws.noaa.gov

*This United Nations agency focuses on meteorology (weather and
climate), operational hydrology, and related geophysical sciences.*
World Meteorological Organization
http://www.wmo.int/pages/index_en.html

Meteorological Equipment Technicians

QUICK FACTS

School Subjects
Mathematics
Technical/shop

Personal Skills
Mechanical/manipulative
Technical/scientific

Work Environment
Indoors and outdoors
Primarily multiple locations

Minimum Education Level
Associate's degree

Salary Range
$31,340 to $50,140 to
$72,840+

Certification or Licensing
Recommended

Outlook
More slowly than the average

DOT
638

GOE
05.02.01

NOC
2241, 2242, 2243

O*NET-SOC
49-2094.00, 49-9069.00

OVERVIEW

Meteorological equipment technicians repair and maintain meteorological equipment that ranges from basic thermometers and barometers to complex technology such as Doppler radar and satellites. Technicians' main duties are to inspect, maintain, repair, and install this equipment. They disassemble equipment to locate malfunctioning components, repair or replace defective parts, troubleshoot electronic circuitry, and reassemble the equipment, adjusting and calibrating it to ensure that it operates according to manufacturers' specifications. Other duties of meteorological equipment technicians include modifying equipment according to the directions of supervisory personnel, arranging with equipment manufacturers for necessary equipment repair (if they are unable to repair the device), and safety-testing instruments to ensure that users are safe from electrical or mechanical hazards. Meteorological equipment technicians work with hand tools, power tools, measuring devices, precision instruments, and manufacturers' manuals.

HISTORY

Ever since the first thermometer, barometer, rain gauge, and other meteorological instruments were constructed, there has been a need for workers to repair these devices when they malfunctioned. Early meteorologists typically would build and repair these instruments themselves, but as the complexity and variety of instruments grew, a need developed for skilled technicians who were specially trained to conduct repairs. The development of complex electronic technology such as Doppler radar and satellites in the 20th century created a need for technicians with even more specialized skills who could work with electrical circuitry and computer software and hardware. Today, technicians are in demand to maintain a wide variety of meteorological instruments and systems.

THE JOB

Meteorological equipment technicians repair, calibrate, and maintain a vast array of meteorological instruments, including anemometers, barographs, barometers, ceilometers, hygrometers, lightning detectors, nephoscopes, pyranometers, radiosondes, rain gauges, snow gauges, sunshine recorders, thermographs, thermometers, and weather vanes. They also service Doppler radar systems and satellites.

Repairing faulty instruments is one of the chief functions of meteorological equipment technicians. They investigate equipment problems, determine the extent of malfunctions, make repairs on instruments that have had minor breakdowns, and expedite the repair of instruments with major breakdowns, for instance, by writing an analysis of the problem for the factory. In doing this work, technicians rely on manufacturers' diagrams, maintenance manuals, and standard and specialized test instruments, such as oscilloscopes and pressure gauges.

Installing equipment is another important function of meteorological equipment technicians. They inspect and test new equipment to make sure it complies with performance and safety standards as described in the manufacturer's manuals and diagrams, and as noted on the purchase order. Technicians may also check on proper installation of the equipment, or, in some cases, install it themselves. To ensure safe operations, technicians need a thorough knowledge of the regulations related to the proper grounding of instruments, and they need to actively carry out all steps and procedures to ensure safety.

Maintenance is the third major area of responsibility for meteorological equipment technicians. In doing this work, technicians try to catch problems before they become more serious. To this end, they take apart and reassemble instruments, test circuits, clean and oil moving parts, and replace worn parts. They also keep complete records of all repairs, maintenance checks, and expenses.

In all three of these areas, a large part of technicians' work consists of consulting with meteorologists, engineers, scientists, and other related professionals. For example, they may be called upon to assist a project manager at a weather station as he makes decisions about the repair, replacement, or purchase of new equipment. They consult with research staffs to determine that equipment is functioning safely and properly. They also consult with meteorologists and engineering staffs when called upon to modify or develop instruments or systems. In all of these activities, they use their knowledge of electronics, meteorological terminology, weather phenomena, chemistry, optics, and physics.

Many meteorological equipment technicians work for meteorological equipment manufacturers. These technicians consult and assist in the construction of new instruments and systems, helping to make decisions concerning materials and construction methods to be used in the manufacture of these devices.

REQUIREMENTS

High School

There are a number of classes you can take in high school to help you prepare for this work. Science classes, such as chemistry, earth science, and physics, will give you the science background you will need for working in a scientific environment. Take shop classes that deal with electronics, drafting, or blueprint reading. These classes will give you experience working with your hands, following printed directions, using electricity, and working with computers and machinery. Mathematics classes will help you become comfortable working with numbers and formulas. Don't neglect your English studies. English classes will help you develop your communication skills, which will be important to have when you deal with a variety of different people in your professional life.

Postsecondary Training

To become qualified for this work, you will need to complete postsecondary education that leads either to an associate's degree in instrumentation technology, electronics, or engineering from a two-year institution or a bachelor's degree from a four-year college or university. Most meteorological equipment technicians choose to receive an associate's degree.

In addition to the classroom work, many programs often provide you with practical experience in repairing and servicing equipment in a clinical or laboratory setting under the supervision of an experienced equipment technician. In this way, you learn about electrical components and circuits, the design and construction of common instruments and systems, and computer hardware and software as it applies to meteorological equipment.

By studying various pieces of equipment, you learn a problem-solving technique that applies not only to the instrument studied, but also to instruments you have not yet seen, and even to instruments that have not yet been invented. Part of this problem-solving technique includes learning how and where to locate sources of information.

Some meteorological equipment technicians receive their training in the armed forces. During the course of an enlistment period of four years or less, military personnel can receive training that prepares them for entry-level or sometimes advanced-level positions in the civilian workforce.

Certification or Licensing
Several certifications are offered by the International Society of Certified Electronic Technicians and the Electronics Technicians Association. Contact these organizations for more information.

Other Requirements
Meteorological equipment technicians need mechanical ability and should enjoy working with tools. Because this job demands quick decision making and prompt repairs, technicians should work well under pressure. You should be extremely precise and accurate in your work and enjoy helping others. You should also have good communication skills in order to work well with meteorologists and other technicians.

EXPLORING

You will have difficulty gaining any direct experience in meteorological equipment technology until you are in a training program or working professionally. Your first hands-on opportunities generally come in the clinical and laboratory phases of your education. You can, however, visit school and community libraries to seek out books written about careers in electronics technology and instrument repair. You can also join a hobby club devoted to meteorology, radio equipment, or electronics.

Perhaps the best way to learn more about this job is to set up, with the help of teachers or counselors, a visit to weather station or to arrange for a meteorological equipment technician to speak to interested students, either on site or at a career exploration seminar hosted by your school. You may be able to ask the technician about his or her educational background, what a day on the job is like, and what new technologies are on the horizon. Contact a school offering a program in electronics equipment technology and discuss your career plans with an admissions counselor there. The counselor may also be able to provide you with helpful insights about the career and your preparation for it.

It will also be useful to familiarize yourself with meteorology and meteorological instruments by reading books such as *The American Meteorological Society Weather Book: The Ultimate Guide to America's Weather*, by Jack Williams (Chicago: University of Chicago Press, 2009); *The Atmosphere: An Introduction to Meteorology*, 11th edition, by Frederick K. Lutgens (Upper Saddle River, N.J.: Prentice Hall, 2009); and *Surface Meteorological Instruments and Measurement Practices*, by G. P. Srivastava (New Delhi, India: Atlantic Publishers & Distributors Ltd., 2008).

EMPLOYERS

Meteorological equipment technicians are employed by government agencies (such as the National Oceanic and Atmospheric Administration, the National Aeronautics and Space Administration, the military, and the U.S. Departments of Agriculture, Defense, and Interior, among other agencies). Other technicians are employed by colleges and universities, in private industry, and by research institutes, independent service organizations, and meteorological equipment manufacturers.

STARTING OUT

Most schools offering programs in electronic equipment technology work closely with local industries, and career services counselors are usually informed about openings when they become available. In some cases, recruiters may visit a school periodically to conduct interviews. Also, many schools place students in part-time jobs to help them gain practical experience. Students are often able to return to these employers for full-time positions after graduation.

Another effective method of finding employment is to communicate directly with government agencies, equipment manufacturers, and private companies regarding job openings. Other good sources of leads for job openings include state employment offices, newspaper want ads, and the Web sites of professional associations.

ADVANCEMENT

With experience, meteorological equipment technicians can expect to work with less supervision, and in some cases they may find themselves supervising less-experienced technicians. They may advance to positions in which they serve as instructors, assist in research, or have administrative duties. Although supervisory positions are open to meteorological equipment technicians, some positions are not available without additional education.

EARNINGS

Salaries for meteorological equipment technicians vary in different institutions and localities and according to the experience, training, certification, and type of work done by the technician. According to the U.S. Department of Labor (DOL), the median annual salary for precision instrument and equipment repairers, not otherwise classified was $50,140 in 2009. The top paid 10 percent in this profession made $72,840 or more a year, while the lowest paid 10 percent made less than $31,340 per year. Those in supervisory or senior positions command higher salaries. Depending on their employers, most meteorological equipment technicians enjoy a full complement of benefits, including vacation and sick time as well as holidays and medical and dental insurance.

WORK ENVIRONMENT

Working conditions for meteorological equipment technicians vary according to employer and type of work done. Most technicians generally work a 40-hour week; their schedules sometimes include weekends and holidays, and some technicians may be on call for emergency repairs. Technicians who are employed by equipment manufacturers may have to travel extensively to install or service equipment.

The physical surroundings in which meteorological equipment technicians work may vary from day to day. Technicians may spend most of their time at a workbench repairing equipment or they may have to travel to weather stations and remote sites to repair malfunctioning instruments or systems. Some climbing, bending, stooping, and reaching may be required to repair certain types of equipment.

OUTLOOK

The DOL does not provide an employment outlook prediction for meteorological equipment repairers. It does predict that employment for electrical and electronics installers and repairers of commercial and industrial equipment will grow more slowly than the average for all careers through 2018. Meteorological equipment is becoming more reliable and less prone to breakdown, which will limit employment growth in the field. Technicians who are certified and who have considerable experience repairing and maintaining meteorological equipment will have the best job prospects.

FOR MORE INFORMATION

Contact the following organizations for more information on meteorology:

American Meteorological Society
45 Beacon Street
Boston, MA 02108-3693
Tel: 617-227-2425
E-mail: amsinfo@ametsoc.org
http://www.ametsoc.org

National Weather Association
228 West Millbrook Road
Raleigh, NC 27609-4304
Tel: 919-845-7121
http://www.nwas.org

National Weather Service
1325 East West Highway
Silver Spring, MD 20910-3280
http://www.nws.noaa.gov

World Meteorological Organization
http://www.wmo.int/pages/index_en.html

For information on certification, contact the following organizations:

Electronics Technicians Association
5 Depot Street
Greencastle, IN 46135-8024
Tel: 800-288-3824
E-mail: eta@eta-i.org
http://www.eta-i.org

International Society of Certified Electronics Technicians
3608 Pershing Avenue
Fort Worth, TX 76107-4527
Tel: 800-946-0201
http://www.iscet.org

For information on technician careers and engineering, contact
Junior Engineering Technical Society
1420 King Street, Suite 405
Alexandria, VA 22314-2750
Tel: 703-548-5387
E-mail: info@jets.org
http://www.jets.org

Meteorological Instrumentation Designers

QUICK FACTS

School Subjects
Art
Mathematics

Personal Skills
Artistic
Technical/scientific

Work Environment
Primarily indoors
Primarily one location

Minimum Education Level
Bachelor's degree

Salary Range
$31,810 to $62,540 to
$125,000

Certification or Licensing
None available

Outlook
Little or no change

DOT
142

GOE
01.04.02

NOC
2252

O*NET-SOC
27-1021.00

OVERVIEW

Industrial designers combine technical knowledge of materials, machines, and production with artistic talent to improve the appearance and function of machine-made products. *Meteorological instrumentation designers* are a type of industrial designer who specialize in the creation of weather-measuring devices. Because the science of measuring wind speeds, air pressure, rainfall, and other weather phenomena must be precise, the work of these designers is critical. There are approximately 44,300 industrial designers employed in the United States. Only a small number specialize in designing meteorological instrumentation.

HISTORY

The first meteorological instrument designers were the meteorologists and scientists who decided to try to build devices that would allow them to better conduct research. For example, the Italian physicist Galileo Galilei designed and built an early thermometer in 1593, Italian physicist Evangelista Torricelli designed the barometer in 1643, and German physicist Daniel Fahrenheit designed the mercury thermometer in 1714. In the following centuries, meteorologists, engineers, and other scientists continued to design meteorological instrumentation.

Industrial design developed as a separate and unique profession in the United States in the 1920s (although it had its origins in colonial

America and the industrial revolution). Industrial designers worked closely with engineers, meteorologists, and other scientists to develop sophisticated meteorological technologies such as Doppler radar and weather satellites. Today, industrial designers continue to play a significant role in the design of new meteorological instruments.

THE JOB

Meteorological instruments can range from simple thermometers and rain gauges to computerized, automated weather observing stations. Highly technical designers are also needed by corporations that design and build weather satellites and Doppler radars. In order to design such precise and technical hardware and software, designers must be well versed in meteorological studies and the industry and user requirements for instrumentation.

Some examples of the instruments meteorological instrumentation designers work on include devices you have probably heard of. For example, a rain gauge is a bucket-like instrument that gathers and measures the amount of precipitation over a set time. A thermometer measures temperature. Some device purposes are obvious by their name. Can you guess what a solarimeter measures? This device measures solar radiation levels. A sunshine recorder measures the amount of sunshine at a given location. Other devices are less obvious. For example, have you heard of a hygrometer? This device measures humidity levels. A ceilometer uses a laser or other light source to measure the baseline of cloud formations. A nephoscope measures the direction, velocity, and altitude of clouds.

High-tech instruments have revolutionized the meteorological sciences. Radar, which stands for RAdio Detection And Ranging, was originally developed to detect enemy aircraft. Radar transmitters sent out electronic beams that were reflected back by the metal of an airplane, revealing its location. Similarly it was discovered that water drops in the atmosphere also reflected back radar beams. Soon radar became a valuable tool for detecting and measuring precipitation. A special kind of radar known as Doppler can detect tornadoes and other dangerous kinds of severe weather, measuring wind speed and direction.

Designers also work to create remote-sensing satellites. The first weather satellites were used to take pictures of the earth's surface, illuminating cloud cover. Today's satellites use advanced remote-sensing techniques to measure temperature, winds, and other properties of the atmosphere at many levels. Because they can measure weather conditions in remote areas without a dedicated weather station or even over bodies of water, satellites are an extremely useful tool for monitoring global climate.

Finally, instrumentation designers may work on computer models that simulate days, weeks, and years of atmospheric behavior in minutes or hours. The National Weather Service and most of the world's other weather services produce large-scale weather forecasts by simulating the weather in a computer program.

Regardless of the instrument on which they work, meteorological instrumentation designers must be very precise in their work. Some designers sketch out their designs by hand, but technology has changed the way most meteorological instrumentation designers work. Computer-aided design (CAD) programs allow designers to create electronic designs that they can then test and manipulate. In some cases, a prototype may be built; however, CAD programs now allow engineers to test design features online. Engineers help the designer test for accuracy, precision, performance, strength, durability, and other factors to ensure that the meteorological instrument is sound and meets all technical standards. If the prototype fails the test, the design goes back to the designer for revisions. Once it passes, designs can be sent directly to machine tools that produce three-dimensional models to use as a guide in production. All of these technological advances have decreased the time necessary to design, test, and manufacture meteorological instruments.

REQUIREMENTS

High School

In high school, take as many art and computer classes as possible in addition to college preparatory classes in English, social studies, algebra, geometry, and science (especially physics and earth science). Classes in mechanical drawing may be helpful, but drafting skills are being replaced by the ability to use computers to create graphics and manipulate objects. Science classes, such as physics and chemistry, are also becoming more important as instrumentation designers select materials and components for products and need to have a basic understanding of scientific principles. Shop classes, such as machine shop, metalworking, and woodworking, are also useful and provide training in using hand and machine tools.

Postsecondary Training

A bachelor's degree in fine arts or industrial design is recommended, although some employers accept diplomas from art schools. Training is offered through art schools, art departments of colleges and universities, and technical colleges. Most bachelor's degree programs require four or five years to complete. Some schools also offer a master's degree, which requires two years of additional study. Often, art schools grant a diploma for three years of study in industrial design. Programs in industrial design are accredited by the National Association of Schools of Art and Design.

School programs vary; some emphasize engineering and technical work, while others emphasize an art background. Certain basic courses are common to every school: two-dimensional design (color theory, spatial organization) and three-dimensional design (abstract sculpture, art structures). Students also have a great deal of studio practice, learning to make models of clay, plaster, wood, and other easily worked materials. Some schools even use metalworking machinery. Technically oriented schools generally require a course in basic engineering. Most schools also offer classes in computer-aided design and computer graphics. One of the most essential skills for success as an instrumentation designer is the ability to use design software.

It will also be useful to take a few meteorology-related classes or even earn a degree in the field. You will need to have comprehensive knowledge of weather phenomena in order to design instruments and computer technology that will help meteorologists gather weather data and prepare forecasts.

Other Requirements

Meteorological instrumentation designers are creative, have artistic ability, and are able to work closely with others in a collaborative style. In general, designers do not crave fame or recognition because designing is a joint project involving the skills of many people. In most cases, instrumentation designers remain anonymous and behind the scenes. Successful designers can accept criticism and differences of opinion and be open to new ideas.

EXPLORING

An excellent way to uncover an aptitude for design and to gain practical experience in using computers is to take a computer graphics or a computer-aided design course through an art school, high school program, technical school, or community college. Some community colleges allow high school students to enroll in classes if no comparable course is offered at the high school level. If no formal training is available, teach yourself how to use a popular graphics software program.

Summer or part-time employment at an industrial design firm is a good way to learn more about the profession and what industrial designers do.

You should also examine and use basic meteorological instruments such as rain gauges and thermometers to gain an understanding of how these tools are used. You might be able to take a tour of a weather monitoring facility to observe more complicated technology such as Doppler radar. Ask your science teacher or a counselor to arrange such a tour and perhaps an interview with a meteorological instrumentation designer. If you can't talk to a meteorological instrumentation designer, the next best thing is to interview a general industrial designer about his or her career.

Pursue hobbies such as sculpting, ceramics, jewelry making, woodworking, and sketching to develop creative and artistic abilities. Reading about industrial design can also be very beneficial. Publications such as *Design News* (http://www.designnews.com) contain many interesting and informative articles that describe different design products and report on current trends. This magazine can be found at many public libraries. Read books on the history of industrial design to learn about interesting case studies on the development of specific products. You should also familiarize yourself with meteorology and meteorological instruments by reading books such as *The American Meteorological Society Weather Book: The Ultimate Guide to America's Weather*, by Jack Williams (Chicago: University of Chicago Press, 2009); *The Atmosphere: An Introduction to Meteorology*, 11th edition, by Frederick K. Lutgens (Upper Saddle River, N.J.: Prentice Hall, 2009); and *Surface Meteorological Instruments and Measurement Practices*, by G. P. Srivastava (New Delhi, India: Atlantic Publishers & Distributors Ltd., 2008). Ask your school or community librarian to provide more suggestions.

EMPLOYERS

Approximately 44,300 industrial designers are employed in the United States; only a small number design meteorological instruments. Industrial designers who do not specialize in meteorological instrument design work in all areas of industry. Some specialize in consumer products, such as household appliances, home entertainment items, personal computers, clothing, jewelry, and car stereos. Others work in designing automobiles, electronic devices, airplanes, biomedical products, medical equipment, measuring instruments, or office equipment. Most designers specialize in a specific area of manufacturing and work on only a few types of products.

STARTING OUT

Most employers prefer to hire someone who has a degree or diploma from a college, art school, or technical school. Persons with engineering, architectural, or other scientific backgrounds also have a good chance at entry-level jobs, especially if they have artistic and creative talent. When interviewing for a job, a designer should be prepared to present a portfolio of their work.

Job openings may be listed through a college career services office or in classified ads in newspapers or trade magazines. Qualified beginners may also apply directly to companies that hire industrial designers. Several directories listing industrial design firms can be found in most public libraries. In addition, lists of industrial design firms appear periodically in magazines such as *Bloomberg BusinessWeek* (http://www.businessweek.com) and *Engineering News-Record* (http://enr.ecnext.com). Also, a new industrial designer can read *Getting an Industrial Design Job* at the Industrial Designers Society of America's Web site, http://www.idsa.org.

ADVANCEMENT

Entry-level instrumentation designers usually begin as assistants to other designers. They do routine work and hold little responsibility for design changes. With experience and the necessary qualifications, the designer may be promoted to a higher-ranking position with major responsibility for design. Experienced designers may be promoted to project managers or move into supervisory positions. Supervisory positions may include overseeing and coordinating the work of several designers, including freelancers and instrumentation designers at outside agencies. Some senior designers are given a free hand in designing products. With experience, established reputation, and financial backing, some instrumentation designers decide to open their own consulting firms.

EARNINGS

According to the Industrial Designers Society of America, the average starting salary for industrial designers is $36,000. Designers with five years' experience earn an average of $58,000 a year.

Senior designers with 10 years' experience earn $73,000. Industrial designers with 19 years or more experience earn average salaries of $125,000. Managers who direct design departments in large companies earn substantially more. Owners or partners of consulting firms have fluctuating incomes, depending on their business for the year.

Industrial designers who worked in specialized design services earned mean annual salaries of $62,540 in 2009, according to the U.S. Department of Labor (DOL). Salaries for all industrial designers ranged from less than $31,810 to $95,910 or more.

Instrumentation designers usually receive paid vacations and holidays, sick leave, hospitalization and insurance benefits, and pension programs.

WORK ENVIRONMENT

Instrumentation designers enjoy generally pleasant work conditions. In many companies, the atmosphere is relaxed and casual. Most designers spend a significant amount of time at either a computer workstation or drawing board. Most instrumentation designers work at least 40 hours a week, with overtime frequently required. There is a lot of pressure to speed up the design/development process and get products to market as soon as possible. For some designers, this can mean regularly working 10 to 20 hours or more of overtime a week. Working on weekends and into the evening can be required to run a special computer program or to work on a project with a tight deadline. Designers who freelance, or work for themselves, set their own hours but may work more than 40 hours a week in order to meet the needs of their clients. Meteorological instrumentation designers may occasionally have to travel to outdoor locations to test their prototypes.

OUTLOOK

Employment of all industrial designers is expected to grow about as fast as the average for all occupations through 2018, according to the DOL. This favorable outlook is based on the need to improve product quality and safety, to design new products for the global marketplace, and to design high-technology products. The DOL predicts that designers who combine business expertise with an educational background in engineering and computer-aided design will have the best employment prospects.

Despite the demand for industrial designers, many companies prefer to outsource a significant amount of their work. This is a growing trend within the industry that may make it more difficult for a beginning worker to find an entry-level job. In addition, this is a profession that is somewhat controlled by the economic climate. It thrives in times of prosperity and declines in periods of recession.

The field of meteorological instrumentation design is very small, which means that there are few job openings. Those with advanced education and experience will have the best job prospects.

FOR MORE INFORMATION

Contact the following organizations for more information on meteorology:

American Meteorological Society
45 Beacon Street
Boston, MA 02108-3693
Tel: 617-227-2425
E-mail: amsinfo@ametsoc.org
http://www.ametsoc.org

National Weather Association
228 West Millbrook Road
Raleigh, NC 27609-4304
Tel: 919-845-7121
http://www.nwas.org

National Weather Service
1325 East West Highway
Silver Spring, MD 20910-3280
http://www.nws.noaa.gov

World Meteorological Organization
http://www.wmo.int/pages/index_en.html

For information on opportunities for women in industrial design, contact

Association of Women Industrial Designers
Old Chelsea Station
PO Box 468
New York, NY 10011
E-mail: info@awidweb.com
http://www.awidweb.com

For information on careers and educational programs, and to read Getting an Industrial Design Job, *visit the society's Web site.*

Industrial Designers Society of America
45195 Business Court, Suite 250
Dulles, VA 20166-6717
Tel: 703-707-6000
http://www.idsa.org

For information on accredited design schools, contact

National Association of Schools of Art and Design
11250 Roger Bacon Drive, Suite 21
Reston, VA 20190-5248
Tel: 703-437-0700
E-mail: info@arts-accredit.org
http://nasad.arts-accredit.org

Physical Geographers

OVERVIEW

Geographers study the distribution of physical and cultural phenomena on local, regional, continental, and global scales. *Physical geographers* study the processes that create the earth's physical characteristics, such as weather (including hurricanes and tornadoes), landforms, soils, vegetation, minerals, water resources, and oceans, and the significance of these processes to humans. There are approximately 1,300 geographers employed in the United States.

HISTORY

Geography as a science dates back to the Greek classical period. The early Greeks were the first to expand geography beyond merely mapmaking.

In the 17th century, German geographer Bernhardus Varenius published an important geographic reference titled *Geographia Generalis*, which organized geography into different branches. The first branch examines the form and dimensions of the earth. The second deals with tides, weather variations over time and space, and other factors influenced by the movements of the sun and moon. Together these two branches form the basis of physical geography.

In the mid-19th century, American William Morris Davis introduced a revolutionary concept: physical geological processes are born out of a cycle. According to Davis, the formations of mountains and other landforms are shaped by natural forces such as weather, volcanic eruptions, and other natural processes. Rainfall created rivers that carved V-shaped valleys between mountains. The flow

QUICK FACTS

School Subjects
Earth science
Geography

Personal Skills
Helping/teaching
Technical/scientific

Work Environment
Indoors and outdoors
One location with some
  travel

Minimum Education Level
Bachelor's degree

Salary Range
$39,030 to $71,470 to
  $109,080+

Certification or Licensing
None available

Outlook
Much faster than the average

DOT
029

GOE
02.02.01

NOC
4169

O*NET-SOC
19-3092.00

of rivers shaped landmasses over time, with larger currents carving out wider valleys. Finally, the cycle comes to a close, as the land becomes a flat plain at the lowest elevation possible. The cycle begins again through another natural cause, as another mountain formation is born and the carving process begins again. Although Davis's theory is not entirely accurate, it was unique in its time and helped to modernize geography and create the specific branch of physical geography.

Looking toward the future, technology is changing the landscape of physical geographic research. Due to advanced remote sensing equipment, we can now monitor the earth's resources from airplanes and even outer space via satellites. Physical geographers also use computer-generated geographic information system (GIS) maps to analyze the changes that have occurred in the earth's physical characteristics and predict future changes.

THE JOB

There are two main branches of geography: human geography and physical geography. Human geography is concerned with people and their activities. This includes the fields of transportation, marketing, real estate, urban and regional planning, and tourism. Physical geography is concerned with the surface of the earth and natural processes that occur on it. Physical geographers study different terrain, the distribution of water, climate changes, and the relationships between living organisms. For example, they may investigate how certain animals have adapted to live in particularly harsh or unique environment. These scientists are sometimes confused with geologists. A good way to differentiate the two is to remember that physical geographers are usually more focused on what is on top of the earth's surface rather than what is underneath it.

Physical geography has seen growth in the last few decades because of the acceleration and increased awareness of our negative impact on the environment. These specialists help investigate how humans are influencing nature and how we can minimize our negative impact.

The field of physical geography has a wide scope. As a result, scientists in this field typically specialize in one of many areas. *Biogeographers* research the relationships between plants and animals. *Climatologists* research the effects of weather over long time spans. *Hydrologists* study sources of water and research ways we can protect this critical resource. *Oceanographers* examine the physics and chemistry of oceans. *Pedologists* research the chemical makeup of soils. *Geomorphologists*, or *physiographers*, study the origin and development of landforms and interpret their arrangement and distribution over the earth. *Mathematical geographers* study the earth's size, shape, and movements, as well as the effects of the sun, moon, and other heavenly bodies. Other kinds of physical geographers include *plant geographers, soil geographers*, and *animal geographers*. They study the kinds and distributions of the earth's natural vegetation, soils, and animals. *Cartographers* research data necessary for mapmaking and design and draw the maps.

Regardless of their area of specialty, physical geographers are important because they research processes that concern the human use of the earth. For example, the food we eat requires a special mix of sun, rain, and healthy soil in which to grow. As our human activities slowly shift the expected behavior of the world's climates, agriculture production will be effected, resulting in fewer or poorer quality crops. Physical geographers are prepared to deal with problems of air pollution, water pollution, and the safe disposal of hazardous wastes so they do not affect our land and, as a result, the food we eat.

REQUIREMENTS

High School
Plan on continuing your education after high school, so take your school's college preparatory curriculum. Naturally, you will focus on science classes such as geography and earth sciences. In addition, you will benefit from taking classes in computer science, English, history, and mathematics.

Postsecondary Training
A bachelor's degree with a major in geography is the basic educational requirement for most positions as a professional geographer. Advanced degrees are usually required for most college teaching positions and for those opportunities involving a considerable amount of research activity.

Many colleges and universities offer undergraduate programs in geography. A good number of these institutions also have a curriculum leading to a master's degree or doctorate in geography.

Meteorology courses taken by geography students in a physical geography program might include Microscale Weather and Climate, Urban Meteorology, Synoptic Meteorology and Climatology, Air Pollution Meteorology, Atmospheric Radiation and Remote Sensing, and Methods in Atmospheric Science. Undergraduate study usually includes formal classroom instruction, as well as some field study.

Other Requirements

Prospective geographers need basic skills in statistics and mathematics. They should be able to interpret maps and graphs, express ideas in speech and writing, analyze problems, and make sound judgments.

EXPLORING

Talk to a physical geographer about his or her career. Ask your school counselor to help arrange an information interview. Visit the Web sites of professional geography associations and read books about the field.

There are increasing opportunities to gain experience through college internship programs. A few summer and part-time employment opportunities are available in business or industrial firms. Field experiences, offered as part of the college program, provide the opportunity for potential physical geographers to test their knowledge and personal qualifications.

EMPLOYERS

Approximately 1,300 geographers are employed in the United States. A majority of physical geographers work in local, state or federal government agencies, but they are also employed by nonprofit environmental organizations, colleges and universities, and private industry. A small but growing number of geographers work for map companies, textbook publishers, manufacturers, overseas trading firms, chain stores, market research organizations, real estate developers, environmental consulting firms, travel agencies, banks, and investment firms.

STARTING OUT

Some beginning jobs are available in teaching geography, mostly in secondary schools. However, high school teaching jobs quite often require study in related fields such as social studies, history, or science. Some obtain positions as research or teaching assistants while working toward advanced degrees. Others enter the planning field. Geographers with advanced degrees can qualify for teaching and research positions at the college level. Many consulting jobs also are available.

Each year the federal government has beginning positions in several geography specialties. Interested students should arrange to take the required civil service examination.

ADVANCEMENT

Advancement is dependent on such factors as amount and type of training, experience, and personal interest and drive. Promotions to jobs requiring more skill and competency are available in all specialty areas. Such jobs are characterized by more administrative, research, or advisory responsibilities in environmental planning.

EARNINGS

Earnings and other benefits depend on the amount of training, the nature of the employment situation, and the personal interests and attributes of the individual employee. According to the U.S. Department of Labor (DOL), median annual earnings for geographers were $71,470 in 2009. Salaries ranged from less than $41,930 annually to more than $99,540.

College and university geography teachers earned salaries that ranged from less than $39,030 to more than $109,080 in 2009, according to the DOL. In addition to salaried income, experienced geographers often earn supplemental incomes through consulting, research, and writing activities. Ph.D.'s in industry frequently earn more than those in academia.

Benefits for full-time workers include vacation and sick time, health, and sometimes dental, insurance, and pension or 401(k) plans. Self-employed geographers must provide their own benefits.

WORK ENVIRONMENT

Geographers usually enjoy pleasant working conditions. They spend much of their time in an office or classroom under the typical working conditions of a business, school, or federal agency.

The average workweek of most geographers is 40 hours, particularly for those employed in government or business positions. In some jobs, however, there can be unusual work situations. Fieldwork often requires the geographer to spend an extended period of time living in remote areas, often under primitive conditions.

OUTLOOK

Geography is a very small profession. With the increased emphasis on planning and research in U.S. business and government, however, the number of geographers in business has increased significantly in recent years. According to the *Occupational Outlook Handbook*, employment opportunities for geographers are expected to grow much faster than the average for all occupations through 2018. Competition for college and university teaching jobs is stiff. Many geographers with graduate degrees seek research and management positions in government and private industry. Others fill nonacademic positions in cartography, health services, climatology, flood management, conservation, and environmental planning.

FOR MORE INFORMATION

For maps, books, journals, and other geography-related materials, contact
American Geographical Society
120 Wall Street, Suite 100
New York, NY 10005-3904
Tel: 212-422-5456
E-mail: AGS@amergeog.org
http://www.amergeog.org

To order a copy of the publication Careers in Geography, *visit the AAG Web site.*
Association of American Geographers (AAG)
1710 16th Street, NW
Washington, DC 20009-3198
Tel: 202-234-1450
E-mail: gaia@aag.org
http://www.aag.org

For information on geography education, contact
National Council for Geographic Education
1710 16th Street, NW
Washington, DC 20009-3198
Tel: 202-360-4237
http://www.ncge.org

For information on opportunities for women in geography, contact
Society of Woman Geographers
415 East Capitol Street, SE
Washington, DC 20003-3810
Tel: 202-546-9228
E-mail: swghq@verizon.net
http://www.iswg.org

Physical Meteorologists

OVERVIEW

Physical meteorologists conduct research on the physical and chemical properties of the atmosphere, including solar radiation, cloud formation, and the process of rain creation. They do not gather information for weather forecasts as other meteorologists do, but spend most of their time conducting research. Physical meteorologists are employed by universities and colleges, government agencies, and private environmental companies.

HISTORY

The first major contributions to scientific meteorology in America happened between 1748 and 1775 with Benjamin Franklin's famous experiments regarding lightning and electricity. In his laboratory, Franklin created electric sparks that were smaller but similar to lightning bolts, and proved that there were electric charges in the atmosphere both on cloudy, thunderous days and on sunny days.

Early meteorological research relied on firsthand observations and was limited to what meteorologists saw with the naked eye. It wasn't until the work of John Dalton that meteorological research took a more scientific approach. Though Dalton today is most famous for his discovery of the atom, he was also a meteorology pioneer. Using self-created, primitive instruments that later became the modern-day barometer and thermometer, Dalton kept extensive records beginning in 1787 and spanning 57 years, which measured humidity, temperature, atmospheric pressure, and wind speeds. During this time, he entered more than 200,000 observations. Today,

QUICK FACTS

School Subjects
Earth science
Geography
Physics

Personal Skills
Helping/teaching
Technical/scientific

Work Environment
Indoors and outdoors
One location with some
  travel

Minimum Education Level
Bachelor's degree

Salary Range
$27,431 to $84,710 to
  $127,250+

Certification or Licensing
Recommended

Outlook
Faster than the average

DOT
025

GOE
02.01.01

NOC
2114

O*NET-SOC
19-2021.00

when scientists discuss the earliest existing detailed weather records, they are generally referring to Dalton's records.

Another early meteorologist worth mentioning is James H. Coffin, who studied the origin and movement of winds. In 1840, he built an observatory in Massachusetts that had the first instruments that could record wind variations and pressure changes. For more than 30 years Coffin collected information on the motion of winds and published his famous work, *Winds of the Northern Hemisphere*, in 1853.

Fast forward more than 100 years and you will find the invention of modern tools such as the Doppler radar and the satellite,

Words to Learn

Cold front: The edge of a cold air mass that moves forward and displaces warmer air, leading to dropping temperatures and humidity.

Drought: A period of extremely low or no rainfall—especially one that affects growing conditions for crops or the overall health conditions of humans and animals.

El Niño: Warming of the surface waters along the coast of South America that is associated with dramatic weather changes in that area. Occurring approximately every three to seven years, El Niño can have a ripple effect, causing irregular weather patterns around the world.

Hurricane: A large-scale, fast-moving circulation of winds that moves at a speed of 74 miles per hour or greater. Hurricanes are most common off the western Atlantic Ocean, Caribbean Sea, Gulf of Mexico, or eastern Pacific Ocean.

Jet stream: Strong, high-altitude winds moving in a long and narrow path, traveling at speeds up to 250 miles per hour.

La Niña: Cooling of the surface waters along the coast of South America that alters normal weather patterns around the world. Often occurs after an El Niño event, every three to seven years.

Microburst: A strong and concentrated downward gust of wind that can cause property damage and affect airplane travel.

Thunderstorm: A storm with lightening and thunder. Storms are caused by the rapid movement of warm, moist air into much cooler air.

Tornado: A destructive, funnel-shaped cloud of circular moving air that moves in a narrow path along the ground.

which help measure and track the movement of weather over a wide expanse.

The field of meteorology is increasingly becoming computerized and automated as scientists seek how best to use observations from a wide variety of traditional and new instruments.

THE JOB

Physical meteorologists study the atmosphere, and how chemical and physical variations within its layers affect the transmission of light, energy, and sound and radio waves. Some might focus on the study of atmospheric phenomenon such as severe storms and formation of clouds and precipitation. Research interests of physical meteorologists can be subdivided into five distinct fields.

Atmospheric Electricity. Physical meteorologists are interested in the earth's electromagnetic network and how it is influenced by variations in our atmosphere. They study how atmospheric pressure, wind levels, ice levels in clouds, and even an accumulation of solar particles can have a profound effect on the formation and intensity of atmospheric electricity. Even the smallest variations in the atmosphere play a role in the intensity of lightning storms. Physical meteorologists are also interested in atmospheric electrical phenomena such as the Aurora Borealis and Aurora Australis, which are caused by solar winds.

Cloud Physics. Physical meteorologists research the physical processes that lead to the development of cloud masses. Their study of clouds include how variances in our atmosphere, including pollution or climate changes, can have a profound effect on the water vapor needed for the formation of clouds and the precipitation released from them.

Precipitation Physics. Physical meteorologists are not just concerned with the types of precipitation released from clouds—rain, hail, sleet, or snow—but how the amount and intensity can change depending on the size and type of cloud systems. Scientists use a variety of tools to study precipitation, including aircraft outfitted with cloud chambers to measure temperature, saturation levels, and the height of clouds. Rainmaking experiments conducted by physical meteorologists have benefited large agribusinesses whose livelihoods are dependent on the proper amount of rain during the growing season.

Atmospheric Acoustics. Scientific work regarding this topic includes how the atmosphere affects the transmission of light, sound, and radio waves. The research of physical meteorologists on the variances in atmospheric acoustics may help improve the availability and quality of services such as long-distance communication.

Atmospheric Optics. This is a term for all objects, in the atmosphere and some subjects on the ground, that have color and light—the most common of which is the rainbow. However, physical

A physical meteorologist (*right*) from the National Severe Storm Laboratory, a professor, and a graduate student prepare to launch a tethered weather balloon carrying instruments that measure humidity, temperature, and wind speed. (*Jack Dykinga, Agricultural Research Service, USDA*)

meteorologists study more than just rainbows. They study ice crystal halos, light scattering, and atmospheric refraction, even sunrises and sunsets.

Some physical meteorologists study environmental-related problems such as the depletion of the earth's ozone layer and the greenhouse effect, which are causing global warming.

Physical meteorologists use various tools to conduct research such as remote-controlled small aircrafts and weather balloons equipped with sampling and measuring instruments. These tools are of great value and can provide measurements of atmospheric temperature, pressure, and humidity at different levels of the atmosphere.

Radar equipment, such as Doppler radar, uses electronic beams to probe the atmosphere, and can detect and measure precipitation such as rain, snow, or hail. Meteorologists may also use acoustic sounders to measure the height and speed of winds by releasing sound waves. Satellite images can also be used to provide a glimpse of the earth's surface, including cloud cover density. Satellites are also important tools to gather information over oceans that are not covered by weather stations.

Physical meteorologists rely heavily on the use of high-speed computers to conduct atmospheric research. They can use certain programs that, by running numerical equations repetitively, can simulate days to years of atmospheric occurrences in a matter of minutes. Physical meteorologists use this data to make a weather model for a particular location.

In addition to conducting research, some physical meteorologists teach at colleges and universities. Aside from teaching duties, they may design and supervise research programs, mentor students, and help obtain funding and grants. They also write for publication and present their research findings at seminars and conferences. Travel to various sites and locations is often necessary in this line of work.

REQUIREMENTS

High School

High school courses that will provide good preparation for a career as a physical meteorologist include physics, mathematics, geography, earth science, computer science, chemistry, English, and speech.

Postsecondary Training

You will need at least a bachelor's degree in meteorology, another atmospheric science, or earth science to work as a physical meteorologist. Some students combine a degree in meteorology with a concentration or minor in physics, acoustics, or optics. Many physical meteorologists have advanced degrees. Those who want to teach at the college level should have master's degrees, but preferably doctorates. The American Meteorological Society (AMS) publishes a list of schools that offer degree programs in atmospheric and related sciences at its Web site, http://www.ametsoc.org/amsucar_curricula/index.cfm. Another list of education programs can be found at the National Weather Service's Web site, http://www.srh.noaa.gov/jetstream/nws/careers.htm. Students typically participate in internships as part of their degree requirements. These internships allow them to try out career options and make valuable industry contacts. Visit http://www.ametsoc.org/amsstudentinfo/internships.html for a list of internship opportunities.

Although some beginners in meteorological work have majored in subjects related to meteorology, the usual minimal requirement for work in this field is a bachelor's degree in meteorology. For entry-level positions in the federal government, you must have a bachelor's degree (not necessarily in meteorology) with at least 24 semester hours of meteorology courses, including six hours in the analysis and prediction of weather systems and two hours of remote sensing of the atmosphere or instrumentation. Other required courses include calculus, physics, and other physical science courses, such as statistics, computer science, chemistry, physical oceanography, and physical climatology.

Certification or Licensing
The AMS confers the certified consulting meteorologist designation to meteorologists who meet educational requirements, have at least five years' experience in the field, meet character requirements, and pass an examination. Contact the society for more information.

Other Requirements
To be a successful physical meteorologist, you must have a strong interest in physics, acoustics, and general science. You should also be organized, be able to work as a member of a team, enjoy conducting research and solving problems, have excellent communication skills, and be able to communicate complex theories and weather events both orally and in writing.

EXPLORING

Read books about physical meteorology to learn more about the field. Here is one suggestion: *Physical Principles of Meteorology and Environmental Physics: Global, Synoptic, and Micro Scales*, by David Blake (Hackensack, N.J.: World Scientific Publishing Company, 2008). You should also read books about general meteorology and weather phenomena such as *The American Meteorological Society Weather Book: The Ultimate Guide to America's Weather,* by Jack Williams (Chicago: University of Chicago Press, 2009) and *The Atmosphere: An Introduction to Meteorology,* 11th edition, by Frederick K. Lutgens (Upper Saddle River, N.J.: Prentice Hall, 2009). Ask your school or community librarian to provide more suggestions.

Another good way to learn more about meteorology is to participate in an information interview with a meteorologist. Ask your high school science teacher or counselor to arrange the interview. You can also join science clubs and participate in science competitions to explore meteorology-related topics.

The AMS offers a comprehensive career guide on its Web site, http://www.ametsoc.org/atmoscareers. Content includes suggestions on the types of course work and training to consider during the college years, various career opportunities, typical employers and workplaces, job and salary outlook statistics, and certification information.

EMPLOYERS

Physical meteorologists are employed by colleges and universities, government agencies (such as the National Weather Service, the Department of Defense, and the National Aeronautics and Space Administration), and private companies.

STARTING OUT

Many meteorologists land their first jobs as a result of contacts made during internships or fellowships. Others find positions through college career services offices, from leads provided by college professors, or by direct contact with government agencies and private companies that employ meteorologists. Additionally, the AMS (http://www .ametsoc.org/careercenter) and National Weather Association (http:// www.nwas.org/jobs.php) provide job listings at their Web sites.

ADVANCEMENT

Meteorologists employed by the National Weather Service, the National Aeronautics and Space Administration, and other government agencies advance according to civil service regulations. After meeting certain experience and education requirements, they advance to classifications that provide higher earnings and, often, more responsibility (including supervisory duties). Some physical meteorologists start their own consulting businesses. The normal pattern of advancement for college professors is from instructor to assistant professor, to associate professor, to full professor.

EARNINGS

Median annual earnings of atmospheric scientists (including physical meteorologists) were $84,710 in 2009, according to the U.S. Department of Labor (DOL). Salaries ranged from less than $40,560 to more than $127,250. The average salary for meteorologists employed by the federal government was $94,210.

Meteorologists with a bachelor of science degree are usually hired by the National Weather Service at the GS-5 to GS-7 grade levels; base salaries at these levels ranged from $27,431 (GS-5), to $30,577 (GS-6), to $33,979 (GS-7) in 2010. Those with a master of science degree enter at the GS-7 to GS-9 levels, which had base pay that ranged from $33,979 (GS-7), to $37,631 (GS-8), to $41,563 (GS-9). Meteorologists with Ph.D.'s enter at the GS-9 to GS-11 levels, which ranged from $41,563 (GS-9), to $45,771 (GS-10), to $50,287 (GS-11).

Benefits for meteorologists depend on the employer; however, they usually include such items as health insurance, retirement or 401(k) plans, and paid vacation days.

WORK ENVIRONMENT

Work environments vary depending on job title. Some physical meteorologists spend their entire workdays in front of a computer, conducting research and analyzing weather data. Others spend a considerable amount of time in the field making observations and gathering data. College professors work in comfortable offices and classrooms. They typically teach classes 12 to 16 hours a week, and conduct research, write for publication, grade papers and examinations, and meet with students and other faculty members during the rest of their workday. Professors typically work nine months a year, and have summers off (although some educators spend this time conducting research or teaching classes).

OUTLOOK

There should be good employment for meteorologists in coming years. In fact, the DOL predicts that employment in the field will grow faster than the average for all careers through 2018. Although good job growth is predicted, there will be strong competition for jobs. Physical meteorologists with advanced degrees and certification will have the best employment prospects. Opportunities will be best in private industry.

FOR MORE INFORMATION

For information on geophysics, contact
American Geophysical Union
2000 Florida Avenue, NW
Washington, DC 20009-1277
Tel: 800-966-2481
http://www.agu.org

This organization is a resource for professionals who work in many physics disciplines. For more information, contact
American Institute of Physics
One Physics Ellipse
College Park, MD 20740-3843
Tel: 301-209-3100
http://www.aip.org

Visit the society's Web site for information on careers, certification, and membership and scholarships for college students; a searchable database of postsecondary training programs in meteorology; and answers to frequently asked questions about meteorology.
American Meteorological Society
45 Beacon Street
Boston, MA 02108-3693
Tel: 617-227-2425
E-mail: amsinfo@ametsoc.org
http://www.ametsoc.org

For information on educational requirements and careers, contact
American Physical Society
One Physics Ellipse
College Park, MD 20740-3844
Tel: 301-209-3100
http://www.aps.org

The society offers information on careers, volunteer positions, publications, and internships and jobs for college students. It also offers diversity programs to encourage students of color to enter the field.

American Society of Limnology and Oceanography
5400 Bosque Boulevard, Suite 680
Waco, TX 76710-4446
Tel: 800-929-2756
E-mail: business@aslo.org
http://www.aslo.org

For information on industrial and applied meteorology, contact
National Council of Industrial Meteorologists
PO Box 721165
Norman, OK 73070-4892
Tel: 405-329-8707
E-mail: info@ncim.org
http://www.ncim.org

The National Oceanic and Atmospheric Administration says that its reach "goes from the surface of the sun to the depths of the ocean floor." Visit its Web site for information on environmental topics such as climate monitoring, fisheries management, and coastal restoration, as well as details on careers, summer programs and paid internships for young people, and financial aid for college-level students.

National Oceanic and Atmospheric Administration
1401 Constitution Avenue, NW, Room 5128
Washington, DC 20230-0001
http://www.noaa.gov

Visit the association's Web site for a list of schools with degree programs in meteorology or atmospheric science and information on scholarships and membership for college students.

National Weather Association
228 West Millbrook Road
Raleigh, NC 27609-4304
Tel: 919-845-7121
http://www.nwas.org

The NWS is an agency of the National Oceanic and Atmospheric Administration. Visit its Web site for comprehensive information on weather forecasting and weather phenomena.

National Weather Service (NWS)
1325 East West Highway
Silver Spring, MD 20910-3280
http://www.nws.noaa.gov

This United Nations agency focuses on meteorology (weather and climate), operational hydrology, and related geophysical sciences.
World Meteorological Organization
http://www.wmo.int/pages/index_en.html

Physical Oceanographers

OVERVIEW

Oceanographers study the ocean by conducting observations, surveys, and experiments. *Physical oceanographers* are specialized oceanographers who study physical aspects of the ocean such as temperature and density; tides, waves, and currents; coastal erosion; and the relationship between the ocean and the atmosphere (for example, weather phenomena that affects the oceans such as temperature, wind, and rain).

HISTORY

Ocean currents, tides, winds, and waves have been observed and studied for thousands of years by traders, explorers, and scientists. Many people trace the origins of modern physical oceanography to the work of Matthew Fontaine Maury, a U.S. Navy lieutenant. By analyzing logbooks kept by navy captains, Maury was able to create ocean charts. In 1855, he published *The Physical Geography of the Sea*, the first textbook on oceanography.

Although scientists and explorers had conducted research on the physical and chemical properties of the ocean for hundreds of years before, the ocean expedition of the H.M.S. *Challenger* from 1872–76 marked the first comprehensive study of the sea—especially its lower depths. Expedition scientists traveled to every ocean except the Arctic to gather specimens and samples, take depth soundings, record deep-sea water temperatures, and conduct other research. The *Challenger* expedition allowed scientists to learn more about the oceans of the world than had ever been known.

From 1925–27, a German research expedition aboard the *Meteor* studied the physical oceanography of the Atlantic Ocean. This expedition marked the beginning of the modern age of oceanographic investigation, according to *Invitation to Oceanography*, by Paul R. Pinet.

Today, physical oceanographers continue to conduct research via ocean expeditions, but also rely on technology such as satellites, acoustic measuring devices, underwater vehicles, computer- and satellite-linked floats and buoys, and ocean seismometers (an instrument that measures earth movement on the seafloor).

THE JOB

Physical oceanographers examine physical forces and features within the ocean. They observe and record the currents, temperatures, density, salinity, and acoustical characteristics of the ocean. Physical oceanographers are also concerned with the interaction between the ocean and the atmosphere, land, freshwater sources such as rivers, and the seafloor. A physical oceanographer might, for instance, try to determine how the ocean influences the climate or weather or affects a certain stretch of coastline.

Physical oceanographers gather data via visual observation, shipboard measurements, and programmable computer buoys, satellites, and other technologies. The development of satellites has allowed physical oceanographers to collect data more quickly than in the past. Physical oceanographers also use mathematical modeling software to help answer questions and form hypotheses (an educated guess) about the world's oceans. Some of the issues studied by physical oceanographers include weather and climate trends (including global warming), ocean pollution, the decline of ocean fisheries (which have crashed as a result of overfishing, pollution, and other factors), and algal blooms (often known as red tides) that can harm humans and ocean ecosystems.

Physical oceanographers work closely with biological, chemical, and geological oceanographers; atmospheric scientists; ocean engineers; and other marine scientists to conduct research and solve problems.

Physical oceanographers conduct observational research in the field and assess their findings and conduct experiments in laboratories and offices. Some work as college oceanography professors and write articles and books about their specialty.

REQUIREMENTS

High School

Because a college degree is required for a career in oceanography, you should take four years of college preparatory courses while in high school. Science courses, including geology, biology, and chemistry, and math classes, such as algebra, trigonometry, calculus, and statistics, are especially important to take. Because your work will involve a great deal of research and documentation, take English classes to improve your research and communication skills. In addition, take computer science classes because you will be using computers throughout your professional life. Learning a foreign language will be useful—especially if you plan to work abroad.

Postsecondary Training

A bachelor's degree is the minimum educational requirement to enter the field, but most employers require a master's degree in oceanography, marine science, or a related field. A Ph.D. in oceanography is required for most positions in research and teaching. More than 100 institutions offer programs in marine studies, and more than 35 universities have graduate programs leading to a doctoral degree in oceanography.

Typical classes in a physical oceanography program include Principles of Physical Oceanography, Coastal and Estuarine Oceanography, Fluid Dynamics, Geophysical Fluid Dynamics, Theory of Ocean Circulation, Numerical Modeling in Ocean Circulation, Satellite Oceanography, and Special Topics in Physical Oceanography.

To prepare for graduate work, take mathematics through differential and integral calculus and at least one year each of chemistry and physics, biology or geology, and a modern foreign language.

Many oceanography students participate in internships or work as teaching assistants while in college to gain hands-on experience in the field. A list of internships is available at the American Society of Limnology and Oceanography's Web site, http://www.aslo.org.

Certification or Licensing

Oceanographers may scuba dive when conducting research. Organizations such as PADI provide basic certification (see For More Information for contact details).

Other Requirements

Personal traits helpful to a career in physical oceanography are a strong interest in science, particularly the physical and earth sciences;

an interest in situations involving activities of an abstract and creative nature (observing nature and natural processes, performing experiments, creating objects); an interest in outdoor activities such as swimming or boating; an interest in scholarly activities (reading, researching, writing); and other interests that cut across the traditional academic boundaries of biology, chemistry, and physics. You should have above-average aptitudes in verbal, numerical, and spatial abilities. Other important skills include perseverance, integrity, open-mindedness, and an attentiveness to detail.

EXPLORING

Visit the Sea Grant Marine Careers Web site (http://www.marine careers.net) for information on careers, volunteerships, internships, and other activities, such as sea camps. The Web sites of college oceanography departments offer a wealth of information about the field, typical classes, and internships. You may even be able to contact a professor or department head to ask questions about the career. If you are unable to contact a professor, ask your high school counselor to arrange an information interview with a physical oceanographer. You should also seek opportunities to gain firsthand oceanographic experience. Many coastal universities offer summer camp programs that enable young people to collect and analyze ocean data. You can help pave your way into the field by learning all you can about the geology, atmosphere, and plant and animal life of the area where you live, regardless of whether water is present.

EMPLOYERS

Oceanography jobs can be found all over the United States, and not just where the water meets the shore. Although the majority of jobs are on the Pacific, Atlantic, and Gulf coasts, many other jobs are available to the marine scientist. Universities, colleges, and federal and state agencies are the largest employers of physical oceanographers.

Other employers of physical oceanographers include international organizations, private companies, consulting firms, nonprofit laboratories, and local governments. Sometimes oceanographers are self-employed as consultants with their own businesses.

STARTING OUT

Most college career services offices are staffed to help you find positions with government agencies and in the private sector after you graduate. Often positions can be found through your college's career services office by application and interview. College and university assistantships, instructorships, and professorships are usually obtained by recommendation of your major professor or department chairperson. In addition, internships with the government or private industry during college can often lead to permanent employment after graduation. Additionally, the Marine Technology Society, American Society of Limnology and Oceanography, and The Oceanography Society offer job listings at their Web sites.

ADVANCEMENT

Starting physical oceanography positions for those with a bachelor's degree usually involve working as a laboratory or research assistant, with on-the-job training in applying oceanographic principles to the problems at hand. Some beginning oceanographers with Ph.D.'s may qualify for college teaching or research positions. Experienced personnel, particularly those with advanced graduate work or doctorates, can become supervisors or administrators. Such positions involve considerable responsibility in planning and policymaking or policy interpretation. Those who achieve top-level oceanographer positions may plan and supervise research projects involving a number of workers, or they may be in charge of an oceanographic laboratory or aquarium.

EARNINGS

Salaries for geoscientists (an occupational group that includes geologists, geophysicists, and oceanographers) ranged from less than $43,140 to more than $161,260 in 2009, according to the U.S. Department of Labor (DOL). The median salary was $81,220. Experienced oceanographers working for the federal government earned $94,560 in 2009.

In addition to their regular salaries, oceanographers may supplement their incomes with fees earned from consulting, lecturing, and publishing their findings. As highly trained scientists, oceanographers usually enjoy good benefits, such as health insurance and retirement plans offered by their employers.

WORK ENVIRONMENT

Physical oceanographers conduct research on a research vessel, on a beach, in a laboratory, or at a desk. While oceanographers spend the majority of their time on land analyzing data, many also go to sea at least once or twice each year. One two-week research cruise can provide an oceanographer with enough data to study for an entire year. While at sea, physical oceanographers must live on board a ship in tight quarters with other scientists and support staff. They work in all types of weather—from rough seas caused by storms or high winds, to extreme cold and snow, to blazing sun in tropical regions. Some oceanographers may also conduct research in the ocean by donning scuba gear or journeying to the ocean depths in underwater vehicles.

Physical oceanographers who work in a laboratory or office typically work five-day, 40-hour weeks. They may have to occasionally work longer hours when conducting and observing certain research experiments. Facilities are typically clean and well lit.

Physical oceanographers who work in colleges or universities have a regular school calendar, with summers and breaks off for travel or research.

OUTLOOK

Employment for all geoscientists (including oceanographers) will grow faster than the average for all occupations through 2018, according to the DOL. Despite this prediction, competition for top positions will be strong. Although job availability is difficult to predict for several years out, anyone doing good, solid academic work with a well-known professor in the field will have good employment chances. Additionally, oceanographers who speak a foreign language, have advanced degrees, and are willing to work abroad will have good employment prospects.

FOR MORE INFORMATION

For education and career information, contact the following organizations:

Acoustical Society of America
Two Huntington Quadrangle, Suite 1NO1
Melville, NY 11747-4502
Tel: 516-576-2360
E-mail: asa@aip.org
http://asa.aip.org

American Geophysical Union
2000 Florida Avenue, NW
Washington, DC 20009-1277

Tel: 800-966-2481
http://www.agu.org

The Education section of the institute's Web site has information on careers in biology.

American Institute of Biological Sciences
1444 I Street, NW, Suite 200
Washington, DC 20005-6535
Tel: 202-628-1500
http://www.aibs.org

Visit the society's Web site for information on careers and education.

American Society of Limnology and Oceanography
5400 Bosque Boulevard, Suite 680
Waco, TX 76710-4446
Tel: 800-929-2756
E-mail: business@aslo.org
http://www.aslo.org

For information on oceanography, contact

National Oceanic and Atmospheric Administration
1401 Constitution Avenue, NW, Room 5128
Washington, DC 20230-0001
http://www.noaa.gov

Contact the society for ocean news and information on membership.

The Oceanography Society
PO Box 1931
Rockville, MD 20849-1931
Tel: 301-251-7708
E-mail: info@tos.org
http://www.tos.org

For information on diving instruction and certification, contact

PADI
30151 Tomas Street
Rancho Santa Margarita, CA 92688-2125
Tel: 800-729-7234
http://www.padi.com/scuba

For links to career information and sea programs, visit the following Web sites:

Careers in Oceanography, Marine Science, and Marine Biology
http://ocean.peterbrueggeman.com/career.html

Sea Grant Marine Careers
http://www.marinecareers.net

WomenOceanographers.org
http://www.womenoceanographers.org

Public Policy Experts

QUICK FACTS

School Subjects
Biology
Earth science
English
Government
Speech

Personal Skills
Communication/ideas
Leadership/management
Technical/scientific

Work Environment
Primarily indoors
One location with some
    travel

Minimum Education Level
Master's degree

Salary Range
$40,560 to $84,710 to
    $127,250+

Certification or Licensing
Voluntary

Outlook
About as fast as the average

DOT
025

GOE
02.01.01

NOC
2114

O*NET-SOC
19-2021.00

OVERVIEW

Public policy experts are scientists (including meteorologists) who have extensive training in the social sciences, law, or business. They use this knowledge to help appointed and elected officials develop guidelines and policies for the wise use and protection of natural resources. They also help politicians devise solutions to such environmental problems as global warming and help them develop plans that seek to reduce property damage, injury, and loss of life from tornadoes, hurricanes, floods, and other severe weather events.

HISTORY

It was not until the 20th century that people became serious about issues such as pollution, acid rain, and global warming. Major decisions are being made by politicians regarding how we deal with these issues. Politicians also need information that will help them plan for and address future challenges brought about by severe weather such as tornadoes, hurricanes, drought, and flooding. Public policy experts are meteorologists and other scientists who provide politicians and other governmental officials with scientific information and advice about meteorological and other scientific developments that are affecting or may affect the health and well-being of their constituents. In recent years, their role has grown in importance as our planet faces a growing variety of environmental- and meteorological-based challenges.

THE JOB

Public policy experts are typically scientists (including meteorologists) with special training in business, law, the social sciences, and government. They work with elected and appointed officials to provide information about meteorological events, environmental issues such as global warming and acid rain, and other science-based issues. Many work for politicians in Washington, D.C., or in state capitals. This work is fast-paced when legislative bodies are in session. Public policy experts must prepare reports and talking points summarizing the issue at hand (for example, a dispute about the degree of global warming that is occurring on earth or the role weather plays in the spread of pollution). Public policy experts spend much of their time meeting with people to convince them to support their boss's policy goals, while at the same time listening to the individual's or group's opinions regarding the issue. They meet with constituents, other congressional staff, and staff members of federal or state agencies that may be affected by the legislation.

Other public policy experts work in the private sector for environmental and industry organizations and scientific societies. In environmental and industry organizations, public policy experts follow legislation that is related to their group's goals (for example, fighting global warming, building stronger levees in New Orleans to withstand powerful hurricanes, banning certain chemicals to reduce damage from acid rain, etc.). They work closely with politicians and their staffs to support or oppose legislation that is important to their organization. Public policy experts who are employed by scientific organizations do not argue for or against legislation. Instead, they try to provide objective information to policy makers so that they can make informed decisions about the issue for their constituents. According to the American Society of Limnology and Oceanography, typical issues that a policy expert in this capacity might work on include "funding for scientific research (e.g., National Science Foundation), scientific ethics and guidelines, evolution in the classroom, and working with federal agencies to improve the quality of their science."

Some public policy experts work as legislative affairs specialists for federal agencies whose employees may be required to appear before congressional committees. They prepare agency officials for congressional hearings and briefings by providing them with information about a particular issue. They also answer questions from members of Congress about these issues.

VORTEX2

Sponsored by the National Oceanic and Atmospheric Administration and the National Science Foundation, VORTEX2 bills itself as the largest tornado research project in history. VORTEX2, which stands for Verification of the Origins of Rotation in Tornadoes Experiment, encompasses more than 100 students, scientists, and staff from various colleges and universities around the world collecting data about tornadoes. Because the exact causes of tornadoes are still shrouded in mystery, research gathered by this team is used to enhance cloud models needed for better forecasting and improving tornado warning skills. Thanks to the large size and spread-out locations of VORTEX2 volunteers, researchers for the first time are able to track a tornado from beginning to end.

Questions hoped to be answered by VORTEX2 research include:

- How do tornadoes form?
- What causes the wind to spin in a concentrated funnel form?
- How can we predict the formulation, path, and duration of a tornado?
- Why do some storms cause tornadoes while others do not?

Visit http://www.nssl.noaa.gov/vortex2 for more information.

Public policy experts may also work as *lobbyists*, who try to influence legislators to support legislation that favors certain causes or public interest groups.

REQUIREMENTS

High School

If you would like to become a public policy expert, take as many science and mathematics classes as possible in high school. Since you will frequently interact with constituents, politicians, and congressional staffers, you should take English and speech classes to help hone your communication skills. Other important classes include history, psychology, and computer science.

Postsecondary Training

Public policy experts typically have degrees in meteorology, oceanography, marine science, ocean engineering, earth science, chemistry, biology, geology, or a related field. Some earn dual degrees in one of the aforementioned majors and business, political science, law, or communications. Most public policy experts have a Ph.D. in a science-related field and many years of experience in their profession. Some scientists with a master's degree and considerable experience may be able to find jobs in the field.

Many scientists break into public policy careers by participating in fellowships. For example, those who have completed their Ph.D.'s can participate in the American Association for the Advancement of Science (AAAS) Science & Technology Policy Fellowships (http://fellowships.aaas.org). According to the organization's Web site, the fellowships "help to establish and nurture critical links between federal decision-makers and scientific professionals to support public policy that benefits the well-being of the nation and the planet."

Certification or Licensing

The American Meteorological Society confers the certified consulting meteorologist designation to meteorologists who meet educational requirements, have at least five years' experience in the field, meet character requirements, and pass an examination. Although this certification is not required, it can provide proof that a public policy worker has expertise in the field of meteorology. Contact the society for more information on certification requirements. Other scientific fields also provide voluntary certification programs.

Other Requirements

Public policy experts should be very knowledgeable about their specialty (such as meteorology, chemical oceanography, ocean engineering, or marine biology), have excellent communication skills, be able to work under deadline pressure, have good networking skills, and be able to multitask. They should be good at building coalitions and finding common ground between opposing parties. They also must be ready to work long hours, including nights and weekends when legislative bodies are in session.

EXPLORING

Learn as much as you can about meteorological-oriented policy issues—such as global warming, severe weather planning, acid rain, and pollution—by reading books and visiting Web sites. You can also ask a teacher or counselor to arrange an information interview with a public policy expert about his or career. If you have trouble finding someone to interview, contact science organizations for potential interview leads.

EMPLOYERS

Most public policy experts are employed in Washington, D.C. Others work in state capitals that are located throughout the United States. Policy experts work for legislatures, federal agencies that have an office of legislative affairs, conservation and industry organizations, and scientific societies. Some public policy experts are self-employed.

STARTING OUT

Public policy experts typically enter the field after gaining experience as scientists. Many enter government positions after participating in AAAS Science & Technology Policy Fellowships. Those interested in working in the private sector should contact potential employers directly for information on career opportunities.

ADVANCEMENT

Public policy experts advance by working for larger government agencies or organizations, or by working on more significant issues that are affecting our planet, such as global warming. They also may work as college professors, write books about science, or work as lobbyists.

Public policy experts who work for the federal government advance according to the civil service system.

EARNINGS

According to the U.S. Department of Labor, in 2009, salaries for atmospheric scientists ranged from less than $40,560 to more than $127,250, with a median of $84,710. The average salary for experienced atmospheric scientists working for the federal government was $94,210 in 2009.

Benefits include paid vacation, health, disability, life insurance, and retirement or pension plans.

WORK ENVIRONMENT

Public policy experts often have to work long hours, spending evenings and weekends preparing cases and research materials and interacting with politicians, congressional aides, and others. Government public policy experts may have to spend a considerable amount of time back in the home district of their bosses talking with constituents.

Public policy experts may travel to various places to gather more information about a particular issue via hands-on research or by talking with other scientists and local residents.

OUTLOOK

Employment for public policy experts should continue to be good through the next decade. Politicians need trusted information about global warming, the role of weather in pollution, and countless other scientific topics, and policy experts can provide this information and guidance as they make important decisions.

FOR MORE INFORMATION

Visit the society's Web site for information on careers, certification, and membership and scholarships for college students; a searchable database of postsecondary training programs in meteorology; and answers to frequently asked questions about meteorology.

American Meteorological Society
45 Beacon Street
Boston, MA 02108-3693
Tel: 617-227-2425
E-mail: amsinfo@ametsoc.org
http://www.ametsoc.org

For information on industrial and applied meteorology, contact
National Council of Industrial Meteorologists
PO Box 721165
Norman, OK 73070-4892
Tel: 405-329-8707
E-mail: info@ncim.org
http://www.ncim.org

The National Oceanic and Atmospheric Administration says that its reach "goes from the surface of the sun to the depths of the ocean floor." Visit its Web site for information on careers, summer programs and paid internships for young people, and financial aid for college-level students.

National Oceanic and Atmospheric Administration
1401 Constitution Avenue, NW, Room 5128
Washington, DC 20230-0001
http://www.noaa.gov

Visit the association's Web site for a list of schools with degree programs in meteorology or atmospheric science and information on scholarships and membership for college students.

National Weather Association
228 West Millbrook Road
Raleigh, NC 27609-4304
Tel: 919-845-7121
http://www.nwas.org

The NWS is an agency of the National Oceanic and Atmospheric Administration. Visit its Web site for comprehensive information on weather forecasting and weather phenomena.

National Weather Service (NWS)
1325 East West Highway
Silver Spring, MD 20910-3280
http://www.nws.noaa.gov

This United Nations agency focuses on meteorology (weather and climate), operational hydrology, and related geophysical sciences.

World Meteorological Organization
http://www.wmo.int/pages/index_en.html

Research Meteorologists

OVERVIEW

Research meteorologists study the weather. Using weather models, they can explain why certain types of weather happen, as well as how it affects us and the environment. Computers, weather maps and charts, satellite images, and barometers, thermometers, and rain gauges are just some of the tools research meteorologists use in their work. While most research meteorologists are employed by government agencies, others work for colleges and universities and in private industry.

HISTORY

Meteorological research has been conducted informally for thousands of years. People studied the weather in order to improve crop yields, avoid severe weather such as tornadoes and floods, and simply to better understand the world around them.

In the 16th and 17th centuries meteorological instruments such as the thermometer and barometer were invented that allowed scientists to more accurately gather and study meteorological data. In more recent years, the development of Doppler radar, satellites, and high-speed computers have helped meteorologists and other atmospheric scientists conduct comprehensive research regarding a variety of topics ranging from drought and severe flooding, to tornadoes and thunderstorms, to global warming and air pollution. Research is conducted by meteorologists who work for government agencies such as the National Oceanic and

QUICK FACTS

School Subjects
Earth science
Geography
Physics

Personal Skills
Helping/teaching
Technical/scientific

Work Environment
Indoors and outdoors
One location with some
travel

Minimum Education Level
Bachelor's degree

Salary Range
$27,431 to $84,710 to
$127,250+

Certification or Licensing
Recommended

Outlook
Faster than the average

DOT
025

GOE
02.01.01

NOC
2114

O*NET-SOC
19-2021.00

Atmospheric Administration and the National Aeronautics and Space Administration, colleges and universities, and private companies.

THE JOB

We can't control the weather. We can't stop the rain or snow anymore than we can arrange to have warm and sunny weather every day. However, we can learn a lot about weather and how it affects our lives and our environment—thanks to the work of research meteorologists.

Research meteorologists study past and current weather occurrences to learn why and how certain weather happens. They often work with other specialized scientists, including oceanographers, chemists, hydrologists, biologists, and engineers to study the earth's weather.

Research meteorologists may specialize in either applied or basic research. According to the American Meteorological Society (AMS), applied research focuses mainly on weather and climate observation, analysis, and forecasting. Applied research can be applied to everyday activities and operations such as the development of forecast techniques and methods of verifying forecasts. *Applied research meteorologists* might also study and analyze specific weather phenomena such as the impact of katabatic winds (cold winds that flow down the sides of mountains) on sea-ice cover or the development of monsoons and tropical cyclones in the South China Sea.

Basic research focuses on more fundamental atmospheric processes such as the formation of clouds and precipitation, the circulation of weather on a global scale, and the relationship between weather phenomena and the ocean. The goal of much basic research is to help develop numerical weather prediction models. One of the major research areas of *basic research meteorologists* is global warming. Research meteorologists who are employed by government environmental agencies and private environmental groups study the various causes of global warming. They try to determine the role humans play in global warming and the effects global warming will have on our planet as a whole, as well as on specific regions. Environmentalists cite the work of research meteorologists regarding global warming, acid rain, and other weather-related phenomena when trying to convince lawmakers to pass laws to protect the environment and educate the public about the need to conserve energy, use renewable energy, and generally live lighter on the earth.

Research meteorologists use many different types of tools in their work, including weather maps and charts; computers; and instruments that record temperatures, wind direction and speed,

Words to Learn

Advisory: A report on weather conditions that may lead to hazards, but does not pose immediate dangers.

Atmosphere: The mass of gases that surrounds the earth.

Barometer: An instrument that measures atmospheric pressure.

Climate: The average weather conditions affecting a specific location measured over a long period of time.

Doppler radar: An electronic instrument that measures atmospheric motion of objects such as precipitation.

Heat index: Not the actual temperature, but a number that describes the combination of temperature and humidity.

Isobar: An imaginary line or line on a weather map that connects regions with similar atmospheric pressure.

NEXRAD: Next-generation weather radar; a network of Doppler radars.

Weather modification: Human-initiated attempts to change the weather by using techniques such as cloud seeding.

Wind chill: The cooling effect of the combination of wind and temperature felt by our bodies.

precipitation, and barometric pressure. Research meteorologists also use satellite and radar data to give them information about the movements of storms or wind masses. They rely heavily on computer weather models to make studied inferences on how the weather can have a positive or negative effect on a particular location.

Some research meteorologists, especially those employed at colleges and universities, participate in public outreach programs. They travel to schools, environmental seminars, and conventions to present their findings and give speeches about their work. Some research meteorologists may work as teachers at the secondary and postsecondary levels.

REQUIREMENTS

High School

To prepare for college study, take high school courses in mathematics, geography, computer science, earth science, physics, and chemistry. English and speech courses are also important, since you will need to be good at writing research reports and communicating your findings to coworkers and the public.

Postsecondary Training
You will need at least a bachelor's degree in meteorology to work as a meteorologist. Most research meteorologists have master's degrees or doctorates. For entry-level positions in the federal government, you must have a bachelor's degree (not necessarily in meteorology) with at least 24 semester hours of meteorology courses, including six hours in the analysis and prediction of weather systems and two hours of remote sensing of the atmosphere or instrumentation. Other required courses include calculus, physics, and other physical science courses, such as statistics, computer science, chemistry, physical oceanography, and physical climatology.

The AMS publishes a list of schools that offer degree programs in atmospheric and related sciences at its Web site, http://www.ametsoc .org/amsucar_curricula/index.cfm. Another list of education programs can be found at the National Weather Service's Web site, http://www.srh.noaa.gov/jetstream/nws/careers.htm.

Meteorology students usually participate in one or more internships during their college years. Participating in an internship is an excellent way to learn more about career options, explore your research interests, and make valuable contacts that you may be able to tap when job hunting after graduation. Visit http://www .ametsoc.org/amsstudentinfo/internships.html for a list of internship opportunities.

Certification or Licensing
The AMS confers the certified consulting meteorologist designation to meteorologists who meet educational requirements, have at least five years' experience in the field, meet character requirements, and pass an examination. Contact the society for more information.

Other Requirements
To be a successful research meteorologist, you should, of course, have excellent research skills. What does that really mean? In short, you need to enjoy conducting time-consuming research that may not yield positive results upon the first, second, or even third attempts. You must be highly organized, be attentive to detail, and be able to use meteorological instruments, computer software, and other technology to conduct research. You should also have excellent communication skills and be able to work under deadline pressure.

A meteorologist at the National Center for Atmospheric Research talks about a weather monitor in the operations center that helps pinpoint conditions of heavy freezing drizzle at an airport. If undetected, the freezing precipitation can lead to jet-engine damage. *(Glen Martin,* The Denver Post/*AP Photo)*

EXPLORING

Read books about meteorology such as *The American Meteorological Society Weather Book: The Ultimate Guide to America's Weather,* by Jack Williams (Chicago: University of Chicago Press, 2009). Ask your school or community librarian to provide some other suggestions. Visiting the Web sites of government agencies that conduct meteorological research will provide you with an overview of various research projects. If one attracts your interest, contact meteorologists who are associated with the project for more information. Visit the Web sites of college meteorology programs to learn about degree requirements and typical classes. Contact meteorology associations for information on careers. The American Meteorological Society offers a comprehensive career guide on its Web site, http://www.ametsoc.org/atmoscareers. Content includes suggestions on the types of course work and training to consider during the college years, various career opportunities, typical employers and workplaces, job and salary outlook statistics, and certification information.

EMPLOYERS

Most research meteorologists are employed by federal and state governments. The National Oceanic and Atmospheric Administration (NOAA) is a major employer of research meteorologists. One noteworthy NOAA subagency that employs meteorologists is the Atlantic Oceanographic and Meteorological Laboratory, which houses the Hurricane Research Division, the Climate Diagnostics Center, and the National Severe Storms Laboratory. Other federal employers of research meteorologists include the National Aeronautics and Space Administration, the military, and the U.S. Departments of Agriculture, Defense, and Interior, among other agencies. Other research meteorologists work at colleges and universities and in private industry.

STARTING OUT

College career services offices can provide job leads to meteorology students. Students also obtain job leads via contacts made through internships and fellowships and through relationships developed as a result of membership in professional associations or from attendance at meteorological seminars and workshops. Additionally, the American Meteorological Society (http://www.ametsoc.org/careercenter) and National Weather Association (http://www.nwas.org/jobs.php) provide job listings at their Web sites.

ADVANCEMENT

Research meteorologists advance by earning higher salaries or by being promoted to managerial and supervisory positions. They may also move on from small, state-level agencies to work at major federal agencies that have larger research budgets. Meteorologists who work as college professors receive academic promotions or advance by assuming administrative positions.

EARNINGS

The U.S. Department of Labor reports that median annual earnings of atmospheric scientists were $84,710 in 2009. Salaries ranged from less than $40,560 to more than $127,250. The average salary for meteorologists employed by the federal government was $94,210. Those employed in scientific research and development services earned $87,180.

Meteorologists with a bachelor of science degree are usually hired by the National Weather Service at the GS-5 to GS-7 grade levels;

base salaries at these levels ranged from $27,431 (GS-5), to $30,577 (GS-6), to $33,979 (GS-7) in 2010. Those with a master of science degree enter at the GS-7 to GS-9 levels, which had base pay that ranged from $33,979 (GS-7), to $37,631 (GS-8), to $41,563 (GS-9). Meteorologists with Ph.D.'s enter at the GS-9 to GS-11 levels, which ranged from $41,563 (GS-9), to $45,771 (GS-10), to $50,287 (GS-11).

Depending on their employers, most research meteorologists enjoy a full complement of benefits, including vacation and sick time as well as holidays and medical and dental insurance. Self-employed workers must provide their own benefits.

WORK ENVIRONMENT

Research meteorologists typically work a standard 40-hour week, but may work overtime (including on weekends) to meet project deadlines. They typically work in offices, weather stations, and laboratories, but also conduct field research in remote locations such as the Arctic, deserts, and even beneath the ocean or high atop mountains.

OUTLOOK

Employment for research meteorologists is expected to be strong through 2018. Technological advances have helped meteorologists make a variety of discoveries that allow us to better predict weather phenomena and understand weather-related challenges such as global climate change. Although there will be many new positions for research meteorologists, competition for top jobs will be strong. Opportunities will be best for those with advanced degrees and certification. Employment will be stronger in private industry than at government agencies.

FOR MORE INFORMATION

Visit the society's Web site for information on careers, certification, and membership and scholarships for college students; a searchable database of postsecondary training programs in meteorology; and answers to frequently asked questions about meteorology.

American Meteorological Society
45 Beacon Street
Boston, MA 02108-3693
Tel: 617-227-2425
E-mail: amsinfo@ametsoc.org
http://www.ametsoc.org

The society offers information on careers, volunteer positions, publications, and internships and jobs for college students. It also offers diversity programs to encourage students of color to enter the field.

American Society of Limnology and Oceanography
5400 Bosque Boulevard, Suite 680
Waco, TX 76710-4446
Tel: 800-929-2756
E-mail: business@aslo.org
http://www.aslo.org

For information on atmospheric research, contact
National Center for Atmospheric Research
PO Box 3000
Boulder, CO 80307-3000
Tel: 303-497-1000
http://www.ncar.ucar.edu

For information on industrial and applied meteorology, contact
National Council of Industrial Meteorologists
PO Box 721165
Norman, OK 73070-4892
Tel: 405-329-8707
E-mail: info@ncim.org
http://www.ncim.org

The National Oceanic and Atmospheric Administration says that its reach "goes from the surface of the sun to the depths of the ocean floor." Visit its Web site for information on environmental topics such as climate monitoring, fisheries management, and coastal restoration, as well as details on careers, summer programs and paid internships for young people, and financial aid for college-level students.

National Oceanic and Atmospheric Administration
1401 Constitution Avenue, NW, Room 5128
Washington, DC 20230-0001
http://www.noaa.gov

Visit the association's Web site for a list of schools with degree programs in meteorology or atmospheric science and information on scholarships and membership for college students.

National Weather Association
228 West Millbrook Road
Raleigh, NC 27609-4304

Tel: 919-845-7121
http://www.nwas.org

The NWS is an agency of the National Oceanic and Atmospheric Administration. Visit its Web site for comprehensive information on weather forecasting and weather phenomena.
National Weather Service (NWS)
1325 East West Highway
Silver Spring, MD 20910-3280
http://www.nws.noaa.gov

This United Nations agency focuses on meteorology (weather and climate), operational hydrology, and related geophysical sciences.
World Meteorological Organization
http://www.wmo.int/pages/index_en.html

INTERVIEW

Dr. Thomas A. Schroeder is the chair of the Department of Meteorology at the University of Hawaii and the director of the Joint Institute for Marine and Atmospheric Research. He discussed his career and the field of meteorology with the editors of Careers in Focus: Meteorology.

Q. Can you please tell us a little about yourself, your research interests, and the Joint Institute for Marine and Atmospheric Research?

A. I began as a severe local storms researcher in the 1970s. Since I have been in Hawaii, I have pursued a variety of local and Pacific Basin concerns, ranging from local weather to alternative energy developments (wind and solar). Having a liberal arts background (undergraduate) I have been especially concerned about impacts of weather and climate on society. Since 1994 I have led a center devoted to providing climate services to the Pacific Islands affiliated with the United States [Pacific ENSO Applications Center (PEAC)].

PEAC is one program within the Joint Institute for Marine and Atmospheric Research (JIMAR) at the University of Hawaii at Manoa. JIMAR supports National Oceanic and Atmospheric Administration (NOAA) research in a broad range of themes, including tropical weather and climate, tsunami research, fisheries oceanography, and coastal processes.

Q. Can you tell us about your program?

A. The University of Hawaii Department of Meteorology offers degrees from the B.S. through M.S. and Ph.D. Our undergraduate degree includes substantial flexibility in electives, allowing students to prepare for several career paths. Our undergraduates and M.S. students often serve in a variety of cooperative positions with the National Weather Forecast, Honolulu, which is located on our campus in the same building. We also serve military students from the Joint Typhoon Warning Center, Pearl Harbor.

Students have plentiful opportunities to work on research projects within the department, JIMAR, and the International Pacific Research Center, a joint Japan–U.S. climate research center also at the University of Hawaii. Our students also have opportunities to go to sea on our university research vessels.

Q. What do you like most and least about being a meteorology professor and a meteorologist?

A. What I like best is interacting with students and the public. Weather and climate are real-time issues. There is never a shortage of subject matter. I have had a variety of unusual opportunities, including advising Polynesian noninstrument voyaging, providing television commentary during natural disasters (Hurricane Iniki), tornado chasing (decades before *Twister*), and reviewing insurance risk models.

One of my disappointments is dealing with the numbers of disinterested students I encounter in service courses—the science-for-poets courses. Even our majors don't show tremendous intellectual curiosity. Also, as a chairman and director I have to deal with multiple bureaucracies, which can be very frustrating.

Q. What is one thing that young people may not know about a career in meteorology?

A. My one thing is actually a fairly broad issue. Most young people have a very limited view of the field and the benefits of a solid undergraduate education. When I meet prospective students I often ask them what they aspire to be. Formulaically they discuss either 1) weather forecaster or 2) broadcast meteorologist. They are surprised when I point to the growing private sector (on the order of 40 percent of the membership of the American Meteorological Society).

Additionally, they fail to recognize the quantitative nature (think calculus) of the field. They also are unaware that the ticket to [employment with] the National Weather Service is de facto the M.S. rather than the B.S. They also fail to realize that a basic degree in meteorology prepares them for a variety of opportunities outside the field.

Q. What are the most important personal and professional qualities for meteorologists?

A. Professional qualities include pride in and appreciation of the responsibility associated with the positions, especially on-duty forecasters. In all venues (private and public sectors) critical skeptical thinking is essential. We deal with many subjects that have substantial consequences for society. Meteorology is a science and operates by the rules of science. We need to remember to think as scientists.

Q. What is the employment outlook for meteorologists? Have certain areas of this field been especially promising in recent years?

A. Over my career (40 years) there has been a decent balance between supply and demand. The largest growth area has been in the private sector, especially financial markets (think weather derivatives, risk insurance) as well as software and technology. A combination of immigration restrictions post-9/11 and failure of American secondary education in technical areas may cause a shortage in quality academics and researchers in the near future. NOAA, for one, is concerned about the next generation of NOAA scientists. Sitting as I do at a Pacific basin, internationally focused institution, the diminished numbers of both qualified American and international graduate degree applicants is stunning and worrisome.

Science Writers and Editors

OVERVIEW

Science writers translate technical scientific information so it can be disseminated to the general public and professionals in the field. They research, interpret, write, and edit scientific information. Their work often appears in books, technical studies and reports, magazine and trade journal articles, newspapers, company newsletters, and on Web sites and may be used for radio and television broadcasts. Other science writers work as *public information officers* for government science agencies and museums, zoos, and aquariums.

Science editors perform a wide range of functions, but their primary responsibility is to ensure that text provided by science writers is suitable in content, format, and style for the intended audiences. Readers are an editor's first priority.

HISTORY

The skill of writing has existed for thousands of years. Papyrus fragments with writing by ancient Egyptians date from about 3000 B.C., and archaeological findings show that the Chinese had developed books by about 1300 B.C.

The history of book editing is tied closely to the history of the book and bookmaking and the history of the printing process. In the early days of publishing, authors worked directly with the printer, and the printer was often the publisher and seller of the author's work. Eventually, however, booksellers began to work directly with the authors and took over the role of publisher. The publisher then became the middleman between author and printer. The publisher worked closely with the author and sometimes acted as the editor; the word *editor*, in fact, derives from the Latin word *edere* or *editum* and means supervising or directing the preparation of text. Eventually, specialists were hired to perform the editing function. These editors, who were also called advisers or literary advisers in the 19th century, became an integral part of the publishing business.

The editor, also called the sponsor in some houses, sought out the best authors, worked with them, and became their advocate in the publishing house. So important did some editors become that their very presence in a publishing house could determine the quality of author that might be published there. The field has grown through the 20th and 21st centuries, with computers greatly speeding up the

Weather Resources on the Internet

Here are some weather- and meteorology-oriented Web sites:

American Meteorological Society: *A Career Guide for the Atmospheric Sciences*
http://www.ametsoc.org/atmoscareers

Hurricane Basics
http://www.nhc.noaa.gov/HAW2/english/basics.shtml

National Hurricane Center
http://www.nhc.noaa.gov

National Weather Service
http://www.nws.noaa.gov

National Weather Service Glossary
http://www.weather.gov/glossary

NOAAWatch
http://www.noaawatch.gov

The Online Tornado FAQ
http://www.spc.noaa.gov/faq/tornado/#About

Weather.com
http://www.weather.com

Weather Underground
http://www.wunderground.com

process by which editors prepare text for the printer or electronic publication.

The broadcasting industry has also contributed to the development of the professional writer. Film, radio, and television are sources of entertainment, information, and education that provide employment for thousands of writers. Today, the computer industry and Internet Web sites have also created the need for more writers.

As our world becomes more complex and people seek even more information, professional writers have become increasingly important. And, as science takes giant steps forward and discoveries are being made every day that impact our lives, skilled science writers are needed to document these changes and disseminate the information to the general public and more specialized audiences.

THE JOB

Science writers usually write for the general public. They translate scientific information into articles and reports that the general public and the media can understand. They might write about global warming and its effects on coastal communities, new developments in tornado detection research, global efforts to fight pollution, and countless other topics. Good writers who cover the subjects thoroughly have inquisitive minds and enjoy looking for additional information that might add to their articles. They research the topic to gain a thorough understanding of the subject matter. This may require hours of research on the Internet; in corporate, university, or public libraries; at laboratories or meteorological research stations; or out in the natural world on a research vessel or in a special armored vehicle that keeps occupants safe as they track a tornado. Writers always need good background information regarding a subject before they can write about it.

In order to get the information required, writers may interview scientists (such as meteorologists, oceanographers, marine biologists, etc.), engineers, politicians, college professors, and others who are familiar with the subject. Writers must know how to present the information so it can be understood. This requires knowing the audience and how to reach them. For example, an article on hailstorms may need graphs, photos, or historical facts. Writers sometimes enlist the help of graphic designers or animators in order to add a visual dimension to their work.

For example, if reporting on tornadoes, writers will need to illustrate the weather conditions that cause a tornado. The public will also want to know what areas of the United States are especially affected by tornadoes, what the warning signs are, and what government agencies are doing to prepare their citizens for future tornadoes. In addition, interviews with scientists and tornado survivors add a personal touch to the story.

Writers usually need to work quickly because news-related stores are often deadline oriented. Because science can be so complex, science writers also need to help the audience understand and evaluate the information. Writing for the Web encompasses most journalistic guidelines, including time constraints and sometimes space constraints.

Some science writers specialize in their subject matter. For instance, a science writer may write only about hurricanes and earn a reputation as the best writer in that subject area.

Some writers may choose to be freelance writers either on a full- or part-time basis, or to supplement other jobs. Freelance science writers are self-employed writers who work with small and large companies, research institutions, or publishing firms on a contract or hourly basis. They may specialize in writing about a specific scientific subject for one or two clients, or they may write about a broad range of subjects for a number of different clients. Many freelance writers write articles, papers, or reports and then attempt to get them published in newspapers, trade, or consumer publications.

Editors work for many kinds of publishers, publications, and corporations. Editors' titles vary widely, not only from one area of publishing to another but also within each area. *Book editors* prepare written material for publication. In small publishing houses, the same editor may guide the material through all the stages of the publishing process. They may work with printers, designers, advertising agencies, and other members of the publishing industry. In larger publishing houses, editors tend to be more specialized, being involved in only a part of the publishing process.

Acquisitions editors are the editors who find new writers and sign them up for new projects. They find new ideas for books that will sell well and find writers who can create the books.

Production editors take the manuscript written by an author and polish the work into a finished print or electronic publication. They correct grammar, spelling, and style, and check all the facts. They make sure the book reads well and suggest changes to the author if it does not. The production editor may be responsible for getting the cover designed and the art put into a book. Because the work is so demanding, production editors usually work on only one or two books at a time.

Copy editors assist the production editor in polishing the author's writing. Copy editors review each page and make all the changes required to give the book a good writing style. *Line editors* review the text to make sure specific style rules are obeyed. They make sure the same spelling is used for words where more than one spelling is correct (for example, grey and gray).

Fact checkers and *proofreaders* read the manuscript to make sure everything is spelled correctly and that all the facts in the text have been checked.

The basic functions performed by *magazine* and *newspaper editors* are much like those performed by book editors, but a significant amount of the writing that appears in magazines and newspapers, or periodicals, is done by *staff writers*. Periodicals often use editors who specialize in specific areas, such as *city editors*, who oversee the work of reporters who specialize in local news, and *department editors*. Department editors specialize in areas such as business, fashion, sports, and features, to name only a few. These departments are determined by the interests of the audience that the periodical intends to reach. Like book houses, periodicals use copy editors, researchers, and fact checkers, but at small periodicals, one or a few editors may be responsible for tasks that would be performed by many people at a larger publication.

REQUIREMENTS

High School

If you are considering a career as a writer or editor, you should take English, journalism, and communication courses in high school. Computer classes will also be helpful. If you know in high school that you want to do scientific writing or editing, it would be to your advantage to take biology, physiology, earth science, chemistry, physics, math, and other science-related courses. If your school offers journalism courses and you have the chance to work on the school newspaper or yearbook, you should take advantage of these opportunities. Part-time employment at newspapers, publishing companies, or scientific research facilities can also provide experience and insight regarding this career.

Postsecondary Training

Although not all writers and editors are college educated, today's jobs almost always require a bachelor's degree. Many writers earn an undergraduate degree in English, journalism, or liberal arts and then obtain a master's degree in a communications field such as writing. A good liberal arts education is important since you are often required to write about many subject areas. Science-related courses (or even pursuing a science-related field, such as meteorology, marine biology, oceanography, or environmental science, as a second major) are highly recommended. You should investigate internship programs that give you experience in the communications department of a corporation, environmental firm, government science agency, or research facility. Some newspapers, magazines, or public relations firms also have internships that give you the opportunity to write and work as an editor.

Some people find that after working as a writer, their interests are strong in the science field and they evolve into that writing specialty. They may return to school and enter a master's degree program or take some additional courses related specifically to science writing. Similarly, science majors may find that they like the writing aspect of their jobs and return to school to pursue a career as a science writer.

Other Requirements

Writers and editors should be creative and able to express ideas clearly, have an interest in science, be skilled in research techniques, and be computer literate. Other assets include curiosity, persistence, initiative, resourcefulness, and an accurate memory. For some jobs—on a newspaper, for example, where the activity is hectic and deadlines short—the ability to concentrate and produce under pressure is essential.

You must be detail oriented to succeed as a writer or an editor. You must also be patient, since you may have to spend hours synthesizing information into the written word or turning a few pages of near-gibberish into powerful, elegant English. If you are the kind of person who can't sit still, you probably will not succeed in these careers. To be a good writer or editor, you must be a self-starter who is not afraid to make decisions. You must be good not only at identifying problems but also at solving them, so you must be creative.

EXPLORING

As a high school or college student, you can test your interest and aptitude in the field of writing and editing by serving as a reporter or writer on school newspapers, yearbooks, and literary magazines. Attending writing workshops and taking writing classes will give you the opportunity to practice and sharpen your skills. Practice editing your own work or the work of friends to get a basic introduction to what it takes to work as an editor.

Community newspapers often welcome contributions from outside sources, although they may not have the resources to pay for them. Jobs in bookstores, magazine shops, libraries, and even newsstands offer a chance to become familiar with various publications. If you are interested in science writing or editing, try to get a part-time job in a research laboratory, interview science writers and editors, and read good science writing in major newspapers such as the *New York Times* or in publications published by major science associations.

Information on writing as a career may also be obtained by visiting local newspapers and publishing houses and interviewing some of the writers and editors who work there. Career conferences and other guidance programs frequently include speakers from local or national organizations who can provide information on communication careers.

Some professional organizations such as the Society for Technical Communication welcome students as members and have special student membership rates and career information. In addition, participation in professional organizations gives you the opportunity to meet and visit with people in this career field.

EMPLOYERS

Many science writers and editors are employed, often on a freelance basis, by newspaper, magazine, and book publishers, and the broadcast industries as well. Internet publishing is a growing field that hires science writers and editors. Science writers and editors are also employed by scientific research companies; government agencies that conduct scientific research and other federal, state, and local government agencies; and research and development departments of corporations. Large colleges and universities often employ science writers and editors in their public relations departments and as writing professors. Zoos, aquariums, museums, and government agencies also employ writers as public information officers.

STARTING OUT

A fair amount of experience is required to gain a high-level position in this field. Most writers start out in entry-level positions. These jobs may be listed with college career services offices, or you may apply directly to the employment departments of publishing companies, corporations, institutions, universities, research facilities, nonprofit organizations, and government facilities that hire science writers. Many firms now hire writers directly upon application or recommendation of college professors and career services offices. Want ads in newspapers and trade journals are another source for jobs. Serving an internship in college can give you the advantage of knowing people who can give you personal recommendations.

Internships are also excellent ways to build your portfolio. Employers in the communications field are usually interested in seeing samples of your published writing assembled in an organized portfolio or scrapbook. Working on your college's magazine or newspaper staff can help you build a portfolio. Sometimes small, regional, or local magazines and newspapers will also buy articles or assign short pieces for you to write. You should attempt to build your portfolio with good writing samples. Be sure to include the type of writing you are interested in doing, if possible.

You may need to begin your career as a junior writer or editor and work your way up. This usually involves library research, preparation of rough drafts for part or all of a report, cataloging, and other related writing tasks. These are generally carried on under the supervision of a senior writer.

Many science writers enter the field after working in public relations departments or science-related industries. They may use their skills to transfer to specialized writing positions or they may take additional courses or graduate work that focuses on writing or documentation skills.

There is tremendous competition for editorial jobs, so it is important for a beginner who wishes to break into the business to be as well prepared as possible. College students who have gained experience as interns, have worked for publications during summer vacations, or have attended special programs in publishing will be at an advantage. In addition, applicants for any editorial position must be extremely careful when preparing cover letters and resumes. Even a single error in spelling or usage will disqualify an applicant. Applicants for editorial or proofreading positions must also expect to take and pass tests that are designed to determine their language skills.

Many editors enter the field as editorial assistants or proofreaders. Some editorial assistants perform only clerical tasks, whereas others may also proofread or perform basic editorial tasks. Typically, an editorial assistant who performs well will be given the opportunity to take on more and more editorial duties as time passes. Proofreaders have the advantage of being able to look at the work of editors, so they can learn while they do their own work.

Good sources of information about job openings are school career services offices, classified ads in newspapers and trade journals, specialized publications such as *Publishers Weekly* (http://publishersweekly.com), and Internet sites. One way to proceed is to identify local publishers through the Yellow Pages. Many publishers have Web sites that list job openings, and large publishers often have telephone job lines that serve the same purpose.

ADVANCEMENT

Writers with only an undergraduate degree may choose to earn a graduate degree in science writing, corporate communications, graphic design, or a related program. An advanced degree may open doors to more progressive career options.

Many experienced science writers are often promoted to head writing, documentation, or public relations departments within corporations or institutions. Some may become recognized experts in their field and their writings may be in demand by trade journals, newspapers, magazines, and the broadcast industry. Writers employed by newspapers and magazines may advance by working for larger, more prestigious publications.

As freelance writers prove themselves and work successfully with clients, they may be able to demand increased contract fees or hourly rates.

In book publishing houses, employees who start as editorial assistants or proofreaders and show promise generally become copy editors. After gaining skill in that position, they may be given a wider range of duties while retaining the same title. The next step may be a position as a *senior copy editor*, which involves overseeing the work of junior copy editors, or as a project editor. The *project editor* performs a wide variety of tasks, including copyediting, coordinating the work of in-house and freelance copy editors, and managing the schedule of a particular project. From this position, an editor may move up to become *first assistant editor*, then *managing editor*, then *editor in chief*. These positions involve more management and decision making than is usually found in the positions described previously. The editor in chief works with the publisher to ensure that a suitable editorial policy is being followed, while the managing editor is responsible for all aspects of the editorial department. The assistant editor provides support to the managing editor.

Newspaper editors generally begin working on the copy desk, where they progress from less significant stories and projects to major news and feature stories. A common route to advancement is for copy editors to be promoted to a particular department, where they may move up the ranks to management positions. An editor who has achieved success in a department may become a city editor, who is responsible for news, or a managing editor, who runs the entire editorial operation of a newspaper.

The advancement path for magazine editors is similar to that of book editors. After they become copy editors, they work their way up to become senior editors, managing editors, and editors in chief. In many cases, magazine editors advance by moving from a position on one magazine to the same position with a larger or more prestigious magazine. Such moves often bring significant increases in both pay and status.

EARNINGS

Although there are no specific salary surveys for science writers, salary information for all writers is available. The U.S. Department of Labor (DOL) reports that the median annual salary for writers was $53,900 in 2009. Salaries ranged from less than $28,070 to more than $105,710. Mean annual earnings for writers employed by newspaper, book, and directory publishers were $53,050 in 2009. Technical writers earned salaries that ranged from less than $37,070 to $100,020 or more.

The DOL reports that the median annual earnings for all editors were $50,800 in 2009. Salaries ranged from $28,430 or less to more than $97,360. Those who worked for newspaper, periodical, book, and directory publishers earned annual mean salaries of $58,580.

Freelance writers' and editors' earnings can vary depending on their expertise, reputation, and the articles they are contracted to write.

Most full-time writing and editing positions offer the usual benefits such as insurance, sick leave, and paid vacation. Some jobs also provide tuition reimbursement and retirement benefits. Freelance writers must pay for their own insurance. However, there are professional associations that may offer group insurance rates for their members.

WORK ENVIRONMENT

The work environment depends on the type of science writing and the employer. Generally, writers work in an office or research environment. Writers for the news media sometimes work in noisy surroundings. Some writers travel to research information and conduct interviews while other employers may confine research to local libraries or the Internet. In addition, some employers require writers to conduct research interviews over the phone, rather than in person.

Although the workweek usually runs 35 to 40 hours in a normal office setting, many writers may have to work overtime to cover a story, interview people, meet deadlines, or to disseminate information in a timely manner. The newspaper and broadcasting industries deliver the news 24 hours a day, seven days a week. Writers often work nights and weekends to meet press deadlines or to cover a late-developing story.

Each day may bring new and interesting situations. Some stories may even take writers to remote and exotic locales. Other assignments may be boring or they may take place in less than desirable settings, where interview subjects may be rude, busy, and unwilling to talk or conditions may be cold, snowy, rainy, or otherwise uncomfortable. One of the most difficult elements for writers may be meeting deadlines or gathering information. People who are the most content as writers work well with deadline pressure.

The environments in which editors work vary widely. For the most part, publishers of all kinds realize that a quiet atmosphere is conducive to work that requires tremendous concentration. It takes an unusual ability to focus to edit in a noisy place. Most editors work in private offices or cubicles. Book editors often work in quieter surroundings than do newspaper editors or quality-control people in advertising agencies, who sometimes work in rather loud and hectic situations.

Even in relatively quiet surroundings, however, editors often have many distractions. A project editor who is trying to do some copyediting or review the editing of others may, for example, have to deal with phone calls from authors, questions from junior editors, meetings with members of the editorial and production staff, and questions from freelancers, among many other distractions.

Deadlines are an important issue for virtually all editors. Newspaper and magazine editors work in a much more pressurized atmosphere than book editors because they face daily or weekly deadlines, whereas book production usually takes place over several months.

In almost all cases, editors must work long hours during certain phases of the editing process. Some newspaper editors start work at 5:00 A.M., others work until 11:00 P.M. or even through the night. Feature editors, columnists, and editorial page editors usually can schedule their day in a more regular fashion, as can editors who work on weekly newspapers. Editors working on hard news, however, may receive an assignment that must be completed, even if work extends well into the next shift.

OUTLOOK

According to the DOL, there is strong competition for writing and editing jobs, and growth in writing careers should occur at an average rate through 2018. Opportunities will be very good for science writers, as continued developments in the field will drive the need for skilled writers to put complex scientific information in terms that a wide and varied audience can understand.

FOR MORE INFORMATION

The ACES is an excellent source of information about careers in copyediting. It organizes educational seminars and maintains lists of internships.

American Copy Editors Society (ACES)
Seven Avenida Vista Grande, Suite B7, #467
Santa Fe, NM 87508-9207
Tel: 415-704-4884
E-mail: info@copydesk.org
http://www.copydesk.org

The ASNE helps editors maintain the highest standards of quality, improve their craft, and better serve their communities. It preserves and promotes core journalistic values. Visit its Web site to read online publications such as Why Choose Journalism? *and* Preparing for a Career in Newspapers.

American Society of News Editors (ASNE)
11690B Sunrise Valley Drive
Reston, VA 20191-1436
Tel: 703-453-1122
http://www.asne.org

For information on membership, contact
Association of Earth Science Editors
http://www.aese.org

For information on careers in science writing, contact
Council for the Advancement of Science Writing
PO Box 910
Hedgesville, WV 25427-0910
Tel: 304-754-6786
http://www.casw.org

To read advice for beginning science writers, visit the NASW Web site.

National Association of Science Writers (NASW)
PO Box 7905
Berkeley, CA 94707-0905
Tel: 510-647-9500
http://www.nasw.org

For information about working as a writer and union membership, contact

National Writers Union
256 West 38th Street, Suite 703
New York, NY 10018-9807
Tel: 212-254-0279
http://www.nwu.org

For information on scholarships and student memberships aimed at those preparing for a career in technical communication, contact

Society for Technical Communication
9401 Lee Highway, Suite 300
Fairfax, VA 22031-1803
Tel: 703-522-4114
E-mail: stc@src.org
http://www.stc.org

For a wide range of resources relating to environmental journalism, contact

Society of Environmental Journalists
PO Box 2492
Jenkintown, PA 19046-8492
Tel: 215-884-8174
E-mail: sej@sej.org
http://www.sej.org

This organization for journalists has campus and online chapters.

Society of Professional Journalists
Eugene S. Pulliam National Journalism Center
3909 North Meridian Street
Indianapolis, IN 46208-4011
Tel: 317-927-8000
http://www.spj.org

Scientific Photographers

OVERVIEW

Photographers take pictures of people, places, objects, and events using a variety of cameras and photographic equipment. They work in the publishing, advertising, public relations, science, and business industries and provide personal photographic services. They may also work as fine artists. *Scientific photographers* are specialized photographers who combine training in science with photographic expertise. They take photographs (and sometimes video) of a vast array of scientific subjects—ranging from meteorological phenomena (such as lightning, hurricanes, and tornadoes); to medical operations, experiments, and procedures; to a vast array of other subjects that are loosely categorized under the general subject area of science. There are approximately 152,000 photographers employed in the United States.

HISTORY

The word *photograph* means "to write with light." Although the art of photography goes back only about 150 years, the two Greek words that were chosen and combined to refer to this skill quite accurately describe what it does.

The discoveries that led eventually to photography began early in the 18th century when a German scientist, Dr. Johann H. Schultze, experimented with the action of light on certain chemicals. He found that when these chemicals were covered by dark paper they did not change color, but when they were exposed to sunlight, they

QUICK FACTS

School Subjects
Art
Earth science
Physics

Personal Skills
Artistic
Communication/ideas
Technical/scientific

Work Environment
Indoors and outdoors
Primarily multiple locations

Minimum Education Level
Associate's degree

Salary Range
$26,487 to $44,076 to
$61,665+

Certification or Licensing
Voluntary

Outlook
About as fast as the average

DOT
143

GOE
01.08.01, 02.05.02

NOC
5221

O*NET-SOC
27-4021.00

darkened. A French painter named Louis Daguerre became the first photographer in 1839, using silver-iodide-coated plates and a small box. To develop images on the plates, Daguerre exposed them to mercury vapor. Daguerreotypes, as these early photographs came to be known, took minutes to expose and the developing process was directly to the plate. There were no prints made.

Although the daguerreotype was the sensation of its day, it was not until the late 1800s that photography began to come into widespread use, when George Eastman invented a simple camera and flexible roll film. After exposing this film to light and developing it with chemicals, the film revealed a color-reversed image, which is called a negative. To make the negative positive (i.e., print a picture), light must be shone though the negative on to light-sensitive paper. This process can be repeated to make multiple copies of an image from one negative.

One of the most important developments in recent years is digital photography. In digital photography, instead of using film, pictures are recorded on microchips, which can then be downloaded onto a computer's hard drive. They can be manipulated in size, color, and shape, virtually eliminating the need for a darkroom.

Scientific photographs were taken as soon as the first cameras were invented in the 1800s. The sun and moon were two of the most popular subjects for early scientific photographers, who were typically scientists who had become skilled at using photographic equipment. The British-born American chemist John Draper is credited with taking the first daguerreotype of the moon in 1840. The first photograph of a tornado was taken by A. A. Adams, who snapped the image of a dissipating tornado on April 26, 1884, near the town of Garnett, Kansas. Today, scientific photographers play a major role in documenting scientific subjects for study by scientists.

THE JOB

Scientific photographers use digital photography to capture images of medical procedures, natural phenomena, military activities (such as the launching of missiles or detonation of bombs), and a variety of other science-related subjects and processes. Their work is found in textbooks, magazines and journals, advertisements for science-related products, Web sites, instructional films, DVDs, videos, television programs, exhibits, lectures and presentations, and computer-assisted learning programs.

Scientific photographers take photographs of objects that can be seen with the naked eye (such as tornadoes, human organs and plants, and the moon and sun) and those that move too quickly or are too small to be viewed without the assistance of special lenses and photographic techniques, invisible radiation and light sources, and specialized photo imaging systems. In addition to standard techniques used by all photographers, scientific photographers also use the following specialized techniques to take photographs: aerial photography, astronomy photography, high-speed photography and photonics, holography, infrared photography, low light-level photography, micro-imaging photofabrication, photographic visualization, photomicrography, photogrammetry, radiography, remote sensing, stereoscopic (3D) photography, time-lapse photography, ultraviolet fluorescence, and underwater photography.

Some scientific photographers write for trade and technical journals, teach photography in schools and colleges, act as representatives of photographic equipment manufacturers, sell photographic equipment and supplies, produce documentary films, or do freelance work.

REQUIREMENTS

High School
While in high school, take as many art classes and photography classes as you can. You can learn about photo editing software and digital photography in photography and computer classes, and business classes will help if you are considering a freelance career. You should also take as many science classes as possible, including earth science, biology, physics, and chemistry.

Postsecondary Training
Scientific photographers may combine a degree in photography with additional training (or even a double major) in science fields such as earth science, meteorology, engineering, medicine, physics, optics, biology, or chemistry. Others have degrees in science fields such as meteorology or biology and take photography classes or have pursued minors or concentrations in photography.

To become a photographer, you should have a broad technical understanding of photography plus as much practical experience with cameras as possible. Take many different kinds of photographs with a variety of cameras and subjects. Learn how to use digital cameras and photo editing software.

Certification or Licensing
The Professional Photographic Certification Commission, which is affiliated with Professional Photographers of America, offers certification to photographers who have had their creative work reviewed

by a panel of judges and passed a written exam that tests their technical expertise. Visit http://www.certifiedphotographer.com for more information. Additionally, specialized certification is available from the BioCommunications Association and the American Society for Photogrammetry and Remote Sensing.

Other Requirements

You should possess manual dexterity, good eyesight and color vision, and artistic ability to succeed in this line of work. You need an eye for form and line, an appreciation of light and shadow, and the ability to use imaginative and creative approaches to photographs or film. Scientific photographers require certain special skills, including knowledge of optics and physics, a patient personality because many scientific shots take a long time to prepare, and strong communication and interpersonal skills because they often have to work with others to set up shots. In addition, scientific photographers should be in good physical condition because much of the specialized photographic equipment that they use is heavy and bulky.

Self-employed (or freelance) photographers need good business skills. They must be able to manage their own studios, including hiring and managing assistants and other employees, keeping records, and maintaining photographic and business files. Marketing and sales skills are also important to a successful freelance photography business.

EXPLORING

Photography is a field that anyone with a camera can explore. To learn more about this career, you can join high school camera clubs, yearbook or newspaper staffs, and community hobby groups, or enter your work in photography contests. You can also seek a part-time or summer job in a camera shop.

Ask your science teacher to arrange an information interview with a scientific photographer. Take as many science-oriented photos as you can to gain experience. Read books and visit Web sites that focus on scientific photography. Here is one book suggestion: *Images from Science 2: An Exhibition of Scientific Photography*, by Andrew Davidhazy and Michael Peres (Rochester, N.Y.: RIT Cary Graphic Arts Press, 2008). You can also view images of the exhibition by visiting http://www.rit.edu/cias/ritphoto/ifs-2008. If you know that you are interested in working in meteorology, you should familiarize yourself with the field by reading books such as *The American Meteorological Society Weather Book: The Ultimate Guide to America's Weather*, by Jack Williams (Chicago: University of Chicago Press, 2009) and *The Atmosphere: An Introduction to Meteorology*, 11th edition, by Frederick K. Lutgens (Upper Saddle River, N.J.: Prentice Hall, 2009). Your school or community librarian can provide additional suggestions.

EMPLOYERS

About 152,000 photographers work in the United States, more than half of whom are self-employed. Scientific photographers are employed by hospitals, research laboratories, medical centers and schools, pharmaceutical companies, publishers of medical and scientific textbooks, and government agencies and the military. Others work as freelancers.

STARTING OUT

Some scientific photographers enter the field as apprentices, trainees, or assistants. Trainees may move lights and arrange backgrounds for a commercial or portrait photographer or motion picture photographer. Assistants spend many months learning this kind of work before they move into a job behind a camera.

Some photographers choose to go into business for themselves as soon as they have finished their formal education. Setting up a studio may not require a large capital outlay, but beginners may find that success does not come easily.

ADVANCEMENT

Full-time scientific photographers advance by receiving pay raises, promotions, and by being assigned to work on more prestigious projects. Those who begin by working for someone else may advance to owning their own businesses.

EARNINGS

Scientific photographers earned median annual salaries of $44,076 in May 2010, according to Salary.com. Those just starting out in the field earned less than $26,487. Very experienced scientific photographers earned more than $61,665.

Self-employed photographers often earn more than salaried photographers, but their earnings depend on general business conditions. In addition, self-employed photographers do not have the benefits that a company provides its employees.

Photographers in salaried jobs usually receive benefits such as paid holidays, vacations, sick leave, and medical insurance.

WORK ENVIRONMENT

Work conditions vary based on the job and employer. Many scientific photographers work a 35- to 40-hour workweek, but freelancers often put in long, irregular hours. Some scientific photographers work in research laboratory settings; others work on aircraft taking aerial photographs; and still others work underwater. For some scientific photographers, conditions change from day to day. One day, they may be photographing an F5 tornado amidst the grasslands of Kansas; the next they may be taking pictures of a microorganism through the eyepiece of a microscope in a laboratory.

Photographers work under pressure to meet deadlines. Freelance photographers have the added pressure of uncertain incomes and have to continually seek out new clients.

For freelance scientific photographers, the cost of equipment can be quite expensive, with no assurance that the money spent will be repaid through income from future assignments.

OUTLOOK

Employment of all photographers will increase about as fast as the average for all occupations through 2018, according to the *Occupational Outlook Handbook*. Opportunities should be good for scientific photographers. There is demand for scientific images of all types. Medical and scientific advances will create a continuing need for skilled photographers to capture scientific images. Although employment should be good for scientific photographers, it is important to remember that this is not a large field and there is strong competition for top positions.

Photography is a highly competitive field. There are far more photographers than positions available. Only those who are extremely talented and highly skilled can support themselves as self-employed photographers. Many photographers take pictures as a sideline while working another job.

FOR MORE INFORMATION

For information on certification, contact
American Society for Photogrammetry and Remote Sensing
5410 Grosvenor Lane, Suite 210
Bethesda, MD 20814-2160

Tel: 301-493-0290
E-mail: asprs@asprs.org
http://www.asprs.org

For information on educational programs, certification, and membership, contact
BioCommunications Association
220 Southwind Lane
Hillsborough, NC 27278-7907
Tel: 919-245-0906
E-mail: office@bca.org
http://www.bca.org

For membership information, contact
Health and Science Communications Association
39 Wedgewood Drive, Suite A
Jewett City, CT 06351-2420
Tel: 860-376-5915
http://www.hesca.org

For information on accredited photography programs, contact
National Association of Schools of Art and Design
11250 Roger Bacon Drive, Suite 21
Reston, VA 20190-5248
Tel: 703-437-0700
E-mail: info@arts-accredit.org
http://nasad.arts-accredit.org

For information on nature photography, contact
North American Nature Photography Association
10200 West 44th Avenue, Suite 304
Wheat Ridge, CO 80033-2840
Tel: 303-422-8527
E-mail: info@nanpa.org
http://www.nanpa.org

This organization provides training, offers certification, publishes its own magazine, and offers various services for its members.
Professional Photographers of America
229 Peachtree Street, NE, Suite 2200
Atlanta, GA 30303-1608
Tel: 800-786-6277
E-mail: csc@ppa.com
http://www.ppa.com

For information on opportunities in photography for women, contact
Professional Women Photographers
511 Avenue of the Americas, #138
New York, NY 10011-8436
E-mail: info@pwponline.org
http://www.pwponline.org

For information on student membership, contact
Student Photographic Society
229 Peachtree Street, NE, Suite 2200
Atlanta, GA 30303-1608
Tel: 866-886-5325
E-mail: info@studentphoto.com
http://www.studentphoto.com

Solar Energy Meteorologists

OVERVIEW

Solar energy meteorologists combine the study of the practical applications of solar energy with the study of atmospheric conditions (especially the properties and energy output of the sun). They are employed by private industry and government agencies that seek to replace or augment traditional energy resources with solar power.

HISTORY

Early research in solar power traces back to 1890, when the French scientist Henri Becquerel discovered the photovoltaic effect, or the ability to convert the sun's rays into electricity. In 1921, Albert Einstein won his only Nobel Prize based on his work with solar power.

It was not until the 1970s that solar energy began to be seriously considered as an energy source as a result of energy shortages. However, the cost to generate solar power far outweighed the cost of traditional energy sources, making large-scale implementation unfeasible.

Thankfully, since 2000, the cost of solar power generation has decreased. Global use has grown more than 25 percent annually over the last decade. At these rates, solar power use doubles at least every four years.

In recent years, the installation of solar panels on homes and office buildings has increased rapidly, especially in countries such as Germany, Japan, Switzerland, and the United States that offer government-subsidized programs. Industrial usage is also growing,

School Subjects
Earth science
Geography
Physics

Personal Skills
Helping/teaching
Technical/scientific

Work Environment
Indoors and outdoors
One location with some
 travel

Minimum Education Level
Bachelor's degree

Salary Range
$27,431 to $84,710 to
 $127,250+

Certification or Licensing
Recommended

Outlook
Faster than the average

DOT
025

GOE
02.01.01

NOC
2114

O*NET-SOC
19-2021.00

especially at sites that are remote and require little power. Examples include transportation signals (such as navigation buoys), lighthouses, aircraft warning lights on structures, and increasingly in road traffic warning signals.

The great benefit of solar power is that it is reliable and requires little maintenance, making it ideal in places that are remote.

Future growth of solar power depends on continued government incentives and improved photovoltaic technology and energy transmission grids that will drive the price of using these renewable resources down and make them competitive with traditional fossil fuels. This cost equalization could happen as early as 2015 or 2016.

THE JOB

Most everyone enjoys a warm, sunny day. The light and warmth from the sun often energizes people, putting them in a good mood, casting a positive light on things around them, and even providing for some a nice tan. But did you know you could use these same sun rays to power a house, factory, or even a whole town? Solar energy meteorologists spend their time analyzing and predicting the sun's position and power to gain the most benefit from this incredible power source. The net result of utilizing solar energy over non-sustainable resources such as oil and coal can save consumers money and also help reduce pollution and environmental degradation.

Because the use of renewable energy is a relatively new concept, the ability to predict and utilize solar power to its greatest extent is highly challenging. An important aspect of solar meteorology is how many different sciences it encompasses. One must have extensive knowledge in the fields of meteorology and environmental science, but also must know how to convert solar rays into energy (physics), how to build solar energy generators (electrical and mechanical engineering), how to finance the creation of one of these systems (economics), and finally, how to utilize the latest technology to accomplish various goals (computer science). Solar energy meteorologists must wear all these hats and apply their knowledge of atmospheric conditions to energy generation, while taking into account the laws of physics and the capabilities of modern engineering.

Most of the world's energy currently comes from oil, coal, and natural gas. These industries are regulated by U.S. and foreign governments. The desire to "go green" is affecting these industries. The expected large-scale integration of renewable energies into the existing energy supply chain will significantly increase the importance of specialists such as solar energy meteorologists.

The use of solar power is limited by meteorological constraints. Factors such as cloud cover and the changing position of the sun cause the strength of solar rays to change rapidly. Hence, the planning, construction, and operation of renewable energy conversion systems (such as solar energy farms) require detailed meteorological knowledge. Actual cloud-dynamics, radiation waves, and precipitation levels are investigated to assess expected energy output.

Many solar energy meteorologists work in private industry as consultants. One of the emerging opportunities in consulting stretches beyond pure meteorological services, such as forecasting or research studies, into the realm of providing support for decision makers in weather-sensitive industries, such as power generation. The specialized knowledge of solar power meteorologists help companies assess and predict demand and output. A significant market segment for meteorological consulting is found with environmental consulting firms that have departments devoted to renewable energy sources. For example, solar energy meteorologists may work for an engineering company that oversees the construction of new solar farms. These scientists may be called upon to locate and assess potential new sites for solar capacitors. Using meteorological observations and topographic analysis of the area and applying model simulations, they help decide where exactly on the sites the solar towers should be built to maximize the power output.

Like weather forecasters, much of their job is in predicting how atmospheric conditions will affect the operations of the solar farm. Before a site is selected and generators are built, solar power meteorologists extensively document the projected output of a proposed farm. Once a location has been selected, solar energy meteorologists provide advice to contractors, landowners, and local, state, and/or federal entities as the energy farm is built.

Once in production, these scientists perform quality control screening of meteorological and solar data to ensure information is accurate and on course with their previously predicted power output. They also must periodically assess the ever-changing atmospheric conditions and make technical suggestions on the modifications of panels and other energy generators for optimal energy production.

In addition to private industry, solar power meteorologists also work for colleges and universities and government agencies such as the National Oceanic and Atmospheric Administration and the U.S. Department of Energy that conduct research in solar energy generation. They may specialize in either applied or basic research. Applied research can be applied to everyday activities and operations, such as the optimum positioning of solar panels to heat a home. This type of research is very specific and deals primarily with solar energy observation, analysis, and forecasting. Included in such research are the development of forecast techniques and forecast verification methods, and the performance of diagnostic and case studies. Applied research may include technique development such as the creation and modification of methodologies used for remote-sensing solar equipment. Basic research addresses more fundamental atmospheric processes such as study of the sun's rays through the formation of clouds and precipitation.

One thing is certain: to remain relevant and successful, solar energy meteorologists must constantly conduct research and be willing to learn about new technologies. These scientists must always search for new techniques, equipment, and software tools to improve the accuracy of their predictions and the effectiveness of capturing and utilizing solar power. Government agencies and private companies rely on their predictions and methodologies to make large financial investments such as the construction of massive solar farms.

REQUIREMENTS

High School
There are many classes that will help prepare you for college and a career as a solar energy meteorologist. These include mathematics, geography, computer science, physics, and chemistry. Be sure to take as many English and speech classes as possible because you will be frequently asked to write reports and discuss your findings with your employer, other meteorologists, engineers, and construction managers.

Postsecondary Training
A bachelor's degree in meteorology or another atmospheric science, earth science, or a related field is the minimum requirement to work as a meteorologist. Advanced graduate training in meteorology and related areas is required for research and teaching positions, as well as for other high-level positions in meteorology. Doctorates are quite common among high-level personnel. Many students augment their training by participating in meteorology-related internships and fellowships. Classes or even a minor or concentration in renewable energy or photovoltaic technology will also be useful for aspiring solar energy meteorologists.

Certification or Licensing
The American Meteorological Society confers the certified consulting meteorologist designation to meteorologists who meet educational

requirements, have at least five years' experience in the field, meet character requirements, and pass an examination. Contact the society for more information on certification requirements.

Other Requirements

Solar energy meteorologists should have excellent communication skills in order to interact well with coworkers and write reports. They should have detailed knowledge of solar energy technology, solar resource modeling software, geographic information systems technology, and scientific programming and data analysis techniques. Other important traits include strong organization skills, the ability to work under deadline pressure, and a willingness to travel to sometimes remote areas to conduct weather and topographical observations. Solar energy meteorologists who are self-employed must have strong business and marketing skills.

EXPLORING

To learn more about solar energy, read books and magazines about the field. *Solar Industry* (http://www.solarindustrymag.com) and *Solar Today* (http://ases.org) are industry trade journals that can provide you with an overview of solar energy issues and trends. *Careers in Renewable Energy: Get a Green Energy Job*, by Gregory McNamee (Masonville, Colo.: PixyJack Press, 2008), is a useful book that offers an overview of renewable energy technologies and career options, including those in solar energy. You can also read books about meteorology such as *The American Meteorological Society Weather Book: The Ultimate Guide to America's Weather*, by Jack Williams (Chicago: University of Chicago Press, 2009). Ask your school or community librarian to provide more suggestions.

Other ways to learn more about a career in solar energy meteorology or other meteorology fields include talking with a meteorologist about his or her career, visiting the Web sites of college meteorology programs, and participating in meteorology-related internships and volunteer opportunities.

EMPLOYERS

Solar energy meteorologists are employed by solar energy companies; engineering, environmental, and construction firms; and government agencies such as the National Oceanic and Atmospheric Administration and the U.S. Department of Energy. They also work as educators and researchers at colleges and universities. Some solar energy meteorologists are self-employed and operate their own consulting businesses.

STARTING OUT

You can enter the field of meteorology in a number of ways. For example, you can find job leads through your college's career services office or via contacts made through internships or fellowships. Many people also contact potential employers directly to learn about potential openings. Additionally, the Solar Energy Industries Association offers job listings at its Web site, http://www.seia.org. Other good resources for job leads include SolarJobs.us (http://www.solarjobs.us) and RenewableEnergyJobs.net (http://www.renewableenergyjobs.net).

ADVANCEMENT

Solar energy meteorologists advance by receiving higher pay and managerial duties, by working on more prestigious or demanding projects, or by opening their own consulting firms. The normal pattern of advancement for college professors is from instructor to assistant professor, to associate professor, to full professor.

EARNINGS

The U.S. Department of Labor (DOL) reports that median annual earnings of atmospheric scientists were $84,710 in 2009. Salaries ranged from less than $40,560 to more than $127,250. The average salary for meteorologists employed by the federal government was $94,210 in 2009.

Meteorologists with a bachelor of science degree are usually hired by the National Weather Service at the GS-5 to GS-7 grade levels; base salaries at these levels ranged from $27,431 (GS-5), to $30,577 (GS-6), to $33,979 (GS-7) in 2010. Those with a master of science degree enter at the GS-7 to GS-9 levels, which had base pay that ranged from $33,979 (GS-7), to $37,631 (GS-8), to $41,563 (GS-9). Meteorologists with Ph.D.'s enter at the GS-9 to GS-11 levels, which ranged from $41,563 (GS-9), to $45,771 (GS-10), to $50,287 (GS-11).

Benefits for meteorologists depend on the employer; however, they usually include such items as health insurance, retirement or 401(k) plans, and paid vacation days.

WORK ENVIRONMENT

Solar energy meteorologists spend a considerable amount of time in offices conducting research, communicating with employers and coworkers via e-mail or the telephone, and preparing reports. They also travel to current and potential job sites to observe and gather information on weather conditions, visit government or private laboratories to collect information for reports, and attend scientific workshops and conferences.

OUTLOOK

There should be good opportunities for meteorologists in coming years. In fact, the DOL predicts that employment for meteorologists will grow faster than the average for all careers through 2018. There should also be good opportunities for solar energy meteorologists, although competition for these sought-after jobs will be strong. Solar energy use is already well established in high value markets such as remote power, satellites, and communications. Industry experts are working to improve current technology and lower costs to bring solar generated electricity, hot water systems, and solar optimized buildings to the public. As solar energy infrastructure continues to grow, there will be more opportunities for solar energy meteorologists.

FOR MORE INFORMATION

Visit the society's Web site for information on careers, certification, and membership and scholarships for college students; a searchable database of postsecondary training programs in meteorology; and answers to frequently asked questions about meteorology.

American Meteorological Society
45 Beacon Street
Boston, MA 02108-3693
Tel: 617-227-2425
E-mail: amsinfo@ametsoc.org
http://www.ametsoc.org

For industry news and updates, publications, conferences, and career opportunities, contact

American Solar Energy Society
4760 Walnut Street, Suite 106
Boulder, CO 80301-2561
Tel: 303-443-3130

E-mail: ases@ases.org
http://www.ases.org

For general information on the renewable energy industry, contact
Energy Efficiency and Renewable Energy
U.S. Department of Energy
Mail Stop EE-1
Washington, DC 20585-0001
Tel: 877-337-3463
http://www.eere.energy.gov

For information on industrial and applied meteorology, contact
National Council of Industrial Meteorologists
PO Box 721165
Norman, OK 73070-4892
Tel: 405-329-8707
E-mail: info@ncim.org
http://www.ncim.org

Visit the association's Web site for a list of schools with degree programs in meteorology or atmospheric science and information on scholarships and membership for college students.
National Weather Association
228 West Millbrook Road
Raleigh, NC 27609-4304
Tel: 919-845-7121
http://www.nwas.org

The NWS is an agency of the National Oceanic and Atmospheric Administration. Visit its Web site for information on weather forecasting and weather phenomena.
National Weather Service (NWS)
1325 East West Highway
Silver Spring, MD 20910-3280
http://www.nws.noaa.gov

For trade news and updates, publications, conferences, and career opportunities, contact
Solar Energy Industries Association
575 7th Street, NW, Suite 400
Washington, DC 20004-1612
Tel: 202-682-0556

E-mail: info@seia.org
http://www.seia.org

This United Nations agency focuses on meteorology (weather and climate), operational hydrology, and related geophysical sciences.
World Meteorological Organization
http://www.wmo.int/pages/index_en.html

Storm Spotters

QUICK FACTS

School Subjects
Earth science
Geography
Physics

Personal Skills
Helping/teaching
Technical/scientific

Work Environment
Primarily outdoors
Primarily multiple locations

Minimum Education Level
Bachelor's degree

Salary Range
$27,431 to $84,710 to
$127,250+

Certification or Licensing
Recommended

Outlook
Faster than the average

DOT
025

GOE
02.01.01

NOC
2114

O*NET-SOC
19-2021.00

OVERVIEW

Storm spotters, also called *storm interceptors*, are trained meteorologists who maintain a visual watch on the development of a dangerous weather event, such as a tornado, and its progression over a specific period of time. The work of storm spotters is important in the research of severe weather, particularly tornadoes, conducted by the National Oceanic and Atmospheric Administration's National Severe Storms Laboratory.

HISTORY

Storm spotters have existed for as long as there have been severe thunderstorms, tornados, hurricanes, and other dangerous weather phenomena. But it was not until the late 1960s and early 1970s that storm spotting became a practice area for meteorologists. During this time, the National Severe Storms Laboratory (NSSL) developed the first Doppler weather radars. According to the NSSL, storm spotters were needed to provide real-time feedback from the field to report what they were seeing in order to help meteorologists "correlate thunderstorm features such as gust fronts, tornadoes, and microbursts with radar images." Until the mid-1980s, the NSSL conducted data-gathering in the field each spring. Today, it only conducts field-based activities when private funding becomes available for research projects. In addition to the NSSL, other government agencies, private weather research firms, and colleges and universities use the service of meteorologists who work as storm spotters.

Learn More About It

Bechtel, Stefan, Tim Samaras, and Greg Forbes. *Tornado Hunter: Getting Inside the Most Violent Storms on Earth*. Washington, D.C.: National Geographic, 2009.

Gaffney, Timothy R. *Storm Scientist: Careers Chasing Severe Weather*. Berkeley Heights, N.J.: Enslow Publishers, 2009.

Hollingshead, Mike, and Eric Nguyen. *Adventures in Tornado Alley: The Storm Chasers*. New York: Thames & Hudson, 2008.

Reed, Jim. *Storm Chaser: A Photographer's Journey*. New York: Abrams, 2009.

Salmon, David. *Tornado Watch: Meteorology of Severe Storms for Spotters, Chasers, and Enthusiasts*. Salt Lake City, Utah: American Book Publishing Group, 2009.

Treaster, Joseph B. *Hurricane Force: In the Path of America's Deadliest Storms*. New York: Kingfisher, 2007.

JOB

In the Hollywood blockbuster *Twister*, the main characters—two National Severe Storms Laboratory (NSSL) meteorologists—drive through the farming towns of Oklahoma in hot pursuit of tornadoes. Their purpose? To release a tornado-analyzing device, nicknamed "Dorothy," into the heart of a twister. Their work is almost foiled by a storm-chasing competitor driven by fame and fortune, instead of science. The main characters happen upon two super cells merging into a mega F5 tornado. They successfully release Dorothy, and as the tornado passes over, save themselves by strapping onto the exposed portion of an underground water pipe.

While the movie provides great action sequences, it is far removed from the reality of storm spotters. Storm spotters working in the field today are trained meteorologists from the NSSL, university-based weather agencies, or private weather research firms. Their purpose is to observe and report severe weather. They work as part of research projects that collect data to better understand and predict severe weather.

The NSSL employs meteorologists who work as storm spotters, as well as students from the University of Oklahoma (where the laboratory is located), and collaborating scientists. Tornadoes are not the only weather phenomena that are researched. Many spotters also keep watch for other kinds of severe weather including windstorms, hurricanes, freezing rain, hail, and severe winter weather.

Examples of an NSSL project are the VORTEX Projects (Verification of the Origins of Rotation in Tornadoes Experiment). Meteorologists and other scientists working on VORTEX and VORTEX2 track tornadoes to learn more about their formation, structure, and intensity in hopes of developing better detection of severe storms. VORTEX2 team leaders monitor regional weather reports to identify locations showing conditions ideal for the formation of tornadoes. Once they pinpoint a location, storm spotters are assigned to particular teams and dispatched to drive to these locations. Some may be assigned to the radar team, which operates mobile Doppler radar systems. Mounted on trucks, these systems are monitored by storm spotters to gauge wind speed and its direction, as well as the amount of rain and hail resulting from the development of the storm. They may also collect readings from remote-controlled planes hovering near the storm. Weather balloons are also used by storm spotters—these hydrogen-filled balloons outfitted with radiosonde instruments take readings on atmospheric pressure, temperature, and humidity.

Storm spotters may also be assigned to work with the mesonet team, which is composed of research vehicles driving in particular patterns—either north/south, or east/west. Each car is top mounted with sensors in order to track the air temperature, pressure, and humidity, and the wind's speed and any changes in direction. Mesonet vehicles also carry small remote-control planes that are tethered to the car's roof. The planes are released when severe weather is located. Each plane holds instruments designed to collect weather data. Storm spotters work in pairs when assigned to the mesonet team; one spotter is designated as the driver, while the other operates the equipment and collects data.

Storm spotters may also be assigned to mount sticknets—tripod-mounted instruments able to collect data such as wind speed, barometric pressure, changes in temperature, and any accumulating precipitation. This team sets up the sticknets in the direct path of the storm, in single or double rows, about a half-mile apart.

Closer to the location of the tornado—about a mile from the approaching storm, storm spotters set up tornado pods which measure wind speed and its direction, as well as the size, distribution, and velocity of precipitation. This set-up is done in single or double rows, with each pod about 100 yards apart. The storm spotters hope that the pods will be in the path of the storm, with the more pods hit, the better the results.

A storm spotter from the University of Oklahoma pauses after photographing twin funnel clouds as they formed east of Palco, Kansas. *(Steven Hausler, Hays Daily News/AP Photo)*

Storm spotters collect data gathered from VORTEX2 and other such projects and send it to the NSSL. There meteorologists and other scientists study measurements in temperature, precipitation, humidity, and wind strength found around and inside a storm to better understand how and why tornadoes form. Their work may eventually lead to better detection of storm buildup, and give longer warnings to the public.

Storm spotters recognize the dangers of severe weather and make every attempt to stay safe at all times. There are many individuals known as *storm chasers* who, while weather enthusiasts, are not professionally trained in this field. Some have contributed their findings to the NSSL, although most work in the field to document severe weather through photographs and video; some even operate storm-chasing tours.

REQUIREMENTS

High School
High school classes that will provide good preparation for a career in meteorology include mathematics, earth science, geography, computer science, physics, chemistry, English, and speech.

Postsecondary Training

You will need at least a bachelor's degree in meteorology or another atmospheric science, earth science, or a related field to work as a meteorologist. Degrees in physics or electrical engineering (especially the study of radar design and fabrication) may also be useful for storm spotters. The National Severe Storms Laboratory reports that nearly all of its meteorologists have master's degrees or doctorates.

For entry-level positions in the federal government, you must have a bachelor's degree (not necessarily in meteorology) with at least 24 semester hours of meteorology courses, including six hours in the analysis and prediction of weather systems and two hours of remote sensing of the atmosphere or instrumentation. Other required courses include calculus, physics, and other physical science courses, such as statistics, computer science, chemistry, physical oceanography, and physical climatology.

Certification or Licensing

The American Meteorological Society confers the certified consulting meteorologist designation to meteorologists who meet educational requirements, have at least five years' experience in the field, meet character requirements, and pass an examination. Contact the society for more information on certification requirements.

Other Requirements

All meteorologists must be organized, have good communication skills, and enjoy conducting research. In addition to these skills, storm spotters must enjoy participating in field research in sometimes dangerous weather conditions such as tornadoes or hurricanes. They must be able to stay calm under pressure and in the face of danger in order to conduct research effectively and communicate with other meteorologists.

EXPLORING

Read books about weather and storm chasing. There are also many Web sites that provide information on storm spotting/chasing. For example, the National Weather Service's Web site, http://www.weather .gov/om/brochures.shtml#storm, provides useful guides for basic and advanced weather spotters and information on volunteer weather-spotting programs. The American Meteorological Society offers a comprehensive career guide on its Web site, http://www.ametsoc.org/ atmoscareers. Finally, you might consider participating in a professionally operated storm-chasing program to get an idea of the challenges and rewards of the field. It is important to remember to never try to undertake storm-spotting expeditions on your own. Severe weather can be extremely dangerous, and conditions can deteriorate rapidly.

EMPLOYERS

Storm spotters are employed by colleges and universities, television stations, private weather research firms, and government agencies (including the National Severe Storms Laboratory, although it does not employ "storm spotters" per se, but meteorologists who occasionally venture into the field to conduct research on severe weather).

STARTING OUT

You can break into the field of meteorology in a number of ways. For example, new graduates may find positions through the career services offices at the colleges and universities where they have studied. Members of the armed forces who have done work in meteorology often assume positions in meteorology when they return to civilian life. In fact, the armed forces give preference in the employment of civilian meteorologists to former military personnel with appropriate experience. Individuals interested in teaching and research careers generally assume these positions upon receiving their doctorates in meteorology or related subjects.

The National Severe Storms Laboratory provides information on job opportunities and answers to frequently asked questions about employment at its Web site, http://www.nssl.noaa.gov/faq/faq_jobs.html.

ADVANCEMENT

Meteorologists employed by government agencies advance according to civil service regulations. With experience and additional educational achievement, they can receive higher salaries and promotion to managerial positions. Meteorologists who are employed in the private sector advance by working at larger companies, by being assigned to more prestigious research projects, and by receiving higher salaries or managerial duties. College teachers advance by moving up the academic ladder: from instructor to assistant professor, to associate professor, to full professor.

EARNINGS

The U.S. Department of Labor reports that median annual earnings of atmospheric scientists (including storm spotters) were $84,710 in 2009. Salaries ranged from less than $40,560 to more than $127,250. The average salary for meteorologists employed by the federal government was $94,210.

Meteorologists with a bachelor of science degree are usually hired by the National Weather Service at the GS-5 to GS-7 grade levels; base salaries at these levels ranged from $27,431 (GS-5), to $30,577 (GS-6), to $33,979 (GS-7) in 2010. Those with a master of science degree enter at the GS-7 to GS-9 levels, which had base pay that ranged from $33,979 (GS-7), to $37,631 (GS-8), to $41,563 (GS-9). Meteorologists with Ph.D.'s enter at the GS-9 to GS-11 levels, which ranged from $41,563 (GS-9), to $45,771 (GS-10), to $50,287 (GS-11).

Employers offer a variety of benefit packages, which can include any of the following: paid holidays, vacations, and sick days; personal days; medical, dental, and life insurance; profit-sharing plans; 401(k) plans; and retirement and pension plans.

WORK ENVIRONMENT

Working as a storm spotter can be exciting, exhilarating, and rewarding. But it can also be dangerous, since spotters must work close to severe weather phenomena such as tornadoes and hurricanes. Dangerous weather can include hail, hail fog, lightning, high winds, driving rain, ice storms, and flooding. In addition, roads can be slippery or obstructed by animals, debris, car wrecks, and other impediments.

Storm-spotting seasons vary by type of weather event. For example, in the United States, the tornado-spotting season begins in spring and lasts throughout the summer and early fall (with the majority of tornadoes occurring between April and June). The Atlantic Ocean hurricane season begins June 1 and ends November 30. The Eastern Pacific Ocean hurricane season begins May 15 and ends November 30. Storm spotters will be particularly busy during these times, and spend the remaining time back in their offices studying data and writing reports about their findings.

OUTLOOK

According to the *Occupational Outlook Handbook*, employment for meteorologists should grow faster than the average for all careers through 2018. Despite this prediction, there will be strong competition for jobs. Opportunities will be best for those with advanced degrees and certification.

FOR MORE INFORMATION

Visit the society's Web site for information on careers, certifi-
cation, and membership and scholarships for college students;
a searchable database of postsecondary training programs in
meteorology; and answers to frequently asked questions about
meteorology.

American Meteorological Society
45 Beacon Street
Boston, MA 02108-3693
Tel: 617-227-2425
E-mail: amsinfo@ametsoc.org
http://www.ametsoc.org

For information on industrial and applied meteorology, contact
National Council of Industrial Meteorologists
PO Box 721165
Norman, OK 73070-4892
Tel: 405-329-8707
E-mail: info@ncim.org
http://www.ncim.org

For information on severe weather, contact
National Severe Storms Laboratory
National Weather Center 120
David L. Boren Boulevard
Norman, OK 73072-7317
Tel: 405-325-3620
http://www.nssl.noaa.gov

Visit the association's Web site for a list of schools with degree pro-
grams in meteorology or atmospheric science and information on
scholarships and membership for college students.

National Weather Association
228 West Millbrook Road
Raleigh, NC 27609-4304
Tel: 919-845-7121
http://www.nwas.org

The NWS is an agency of the National Oceanic and Atmospheric
Administration. Visit its Web site to learn more about weather fore-
casting and weather phenomena.

National Weather Service (NWS)
1325 East West Highway
Silver Spring, MD 20910-3280
http://www.nws.noaa.gov

This United Nations agency focuses on meteorology (weather and climate), operational hydrology, and related geophysical sciences.
World Meteorological Organization
http://www.wmo.int/pages/index_en.html

Index

Entries and page numbers in **bold** indicate major treatment of a topic.

COLLEGE OF MARIN

3 2555 00142489 9

ATE DUE

COLLEGE OF MARIN LIBRARY
COLLEGE AVENUE
KENTFIELD, CA 94904